THE SOUTHERN WAY

CONTENTS

© Kevin Robertson (Noodle Books) and the various contributors 2013
ISBN 978-1-909328-02-0
First published in 2012 by Kevin Robertson
under the **NOODLE BOOKS** imprint
PO Box 279
Corhampton
SOUTHAMPTON
SO32 3ZX
www.noodlebooks.co.uk
editorial@thesouthernway.co.uk

Printed in England by
Berforts Information Press Ltd.

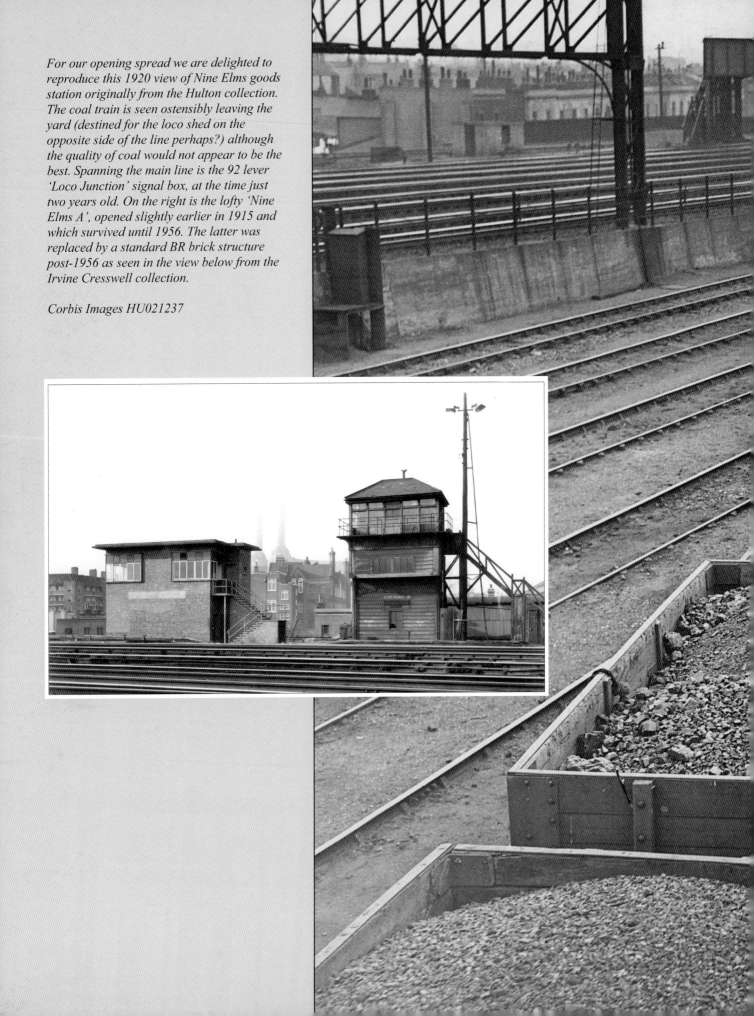

For our opening spread we are delighted to reproduce this 1920 view of Nine Elms goods station originally from the Hulton collection. The coal train is seen ostensibly leaving the yard (destined for the loco shed on the opposite side of the line perhaps?) although the quality of coal would not appear to be the best. Spanning the main line is the 92 lever 'Loco Junction' signal box, at the time just two years old. On the right is the lofty 'Nine Elms A', opened slightly earlier in 1915 and which survived until 1956. The latter was replaced by a standard BR brick structure post-1956 as seen in the view below from the Irvine Cresswell collection.

Corbis Images HU021237

One for the experts. Regular 'Southern Way' contributor, Colin Martin has unearthed (pardon the pun) a small selection of further views showing his father and colleagues at work 'somewhere around Guildford'. Any ideas…? No dates or details are known, whilst what would appear to be going on is a re-adjustment of certain of the platform edge slabs which have moved too close to the track. (Other views in the sequence of four, depict similar work at Clandon and a board / occupation crossing of some sort.)

Front cover - *Eastleigh. Les Elsey.*

Rear Cover - *On 8 September 1962 the LCGB special, which the Beattie tank had been specially retained to operate, is captured at Boscarne Junction with No. 30587 about to make its final outing along the Wenford Bridge branch bringing a distinguished career to an end on this remote Cornish by-way.*

Guest Editorial

Congratulations to Kevin for the first six years' publication of this magazine. He found a niche in the market place which he has exploited with enthusiasm, panache and commercial good sense.

The readership has responded keenly to Kevin's calls for material. To date, there have been some 400 contributors. Of the many excellent articles, however, the SER has had less than its fair share of coverage. This is probably because, other than boat trains, the SER is less evocative than the L&SWR or LB&SCR. Trains did not disperse to the far reaches of the Withered Arm, nor did they criss-cross Surrey and Sussex on myriad secondary lines. So let us redress the balance a bit with a few conundrums relating to the SER. How well can you answer the following:

- To what extent was Charles Dickens a railway enthusiast?

- Which part of the SER main line was engineered by I.K.Brunel?

- Why was St Olave's the only state school in class V?

Charles Dickens wrote about the SER and was a shaken passenger who survived the Staplehurst derailment of 1865. In *The Uncommercial Traveller*, he describes an uncomfortable channel crossing on the deck of a tidal paddle steamer from Dover. In the same book we find a first reference to the British Railways infamous pork pie, the butt of many a jest for a century to come. But he never mentions the North Kent line, the LC&DR or its rivalry with the SER. I believe that Dickens accepted the railways and enjoyed the novelty of train travel. But an enthusiast, I think not. His heart was surely in the age of the stagecoach, exemplified by Pip's journeys on the Rochester road in *Great Expectations*.

The brick piers of Hungerford bridge were engineered by I.K.Brunel. They were built in 1845 for the Hungerford pedestrian suspension bridge. When this was dismantled in 1860, the two piers were retained for the new railway bridge and the wrought iron chains were recycled on the Clifton suspension bridge. Photographs of one of the piers can be found in SW Special Issue No. 3 - *Wartime Southern*. They show 2½ inch cracks caused by a land mine which exploded nearby.

St Olave's was the only school in class V that was not fully independent although that may not have been widely known at the time. Like the SR itself, the school was part-funded by the state from the mid-1920s. Both were taken over by the state in 1948. The school was clearly held in esteem by SR management, perhaps influenced by its proximity to the offices of the SER/ SE&CR/ SR. Or it may have been included in recognition of having to relocate twice due to construction and expansion of the railway viaduct into London Bridge. Or perhaps one of the SR managers had links with the school? We may never know for certain but if you have any further thoughts on the matter, please let Kevin know for his Letters page. Thanks are due to the school for their help and the photograph.

Alan Postlethwaite

Stroud, Gloucestershire, January 2013.

(Alan is a Chartered Engineer who is retired from the electricity industry.)

If you would like to feature as the 'Guest Editor', please contact us in the usual way.

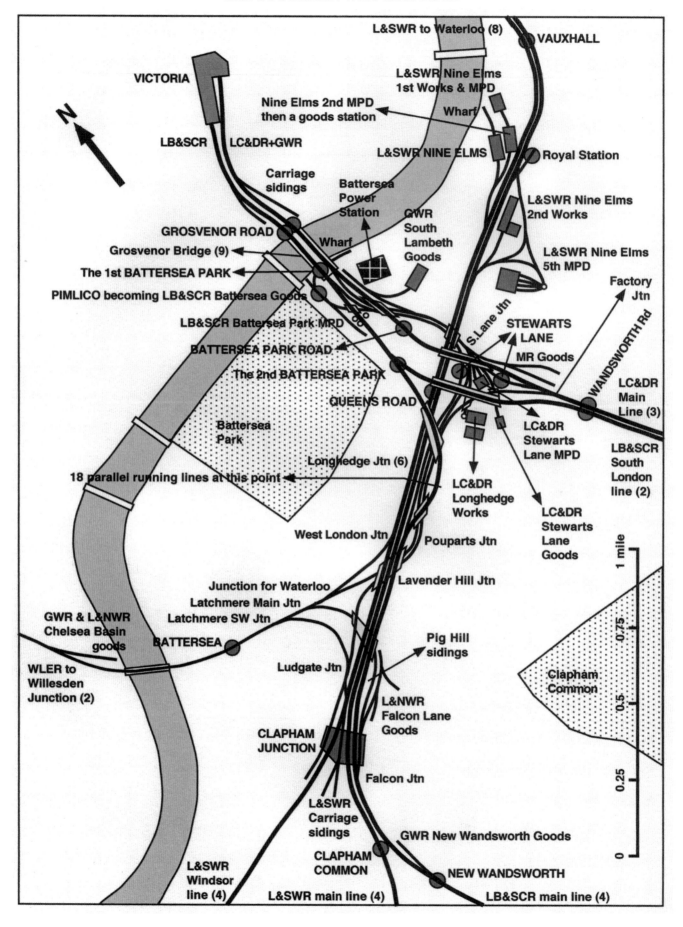

VICTORIA

LB&SCR   LC&DR+GWR

N

Carriage
sidings

L&SWR to Waterloo (8)   VAUXHALL

L&SWR Nine Elms
1st Works & MPD

Nine Elms 2nd MPD
then a goods station

Wharf

L&SWR NINE ELMS   Royal Station

L&SWR Nine Elms
2nd Works

L&SWR Nine Elms
5th MPD

Battersea
Power
Station

GWR
South
Lambeth
Goods

GROSVENOR ROAD

Grosvenor Bridge (9)

The 1st BATTERSEA PARK

PIMLICO becoming LB&SCR Battersea Goods

Wharf

Factory
Jtn

WANDSWORTH Rd

LB&SCR Battersea Park MPD

BATTERSEA PARK ROAD

The 2nd BATTERSEA PARK

QUEENS ROAD

Battersea
Park

Longhedge Jtn (6)

18 parallel running lines at this point

S.Lane Jtn

STEWARTS
LANE

MR Goods

LC&DR
Stewarts
Lane MPD

LC&DR
Main
Line (3)

LB&SCR
South
London
line (2)

LC&DR
Longhedge
Works

LC&DR
Stewarts
Lane
Goods

1 mile

West London Jtn

Pouparts Jtn

Lavender Hill Jtn

GWR & L&NWR
Chelsea Basin
goods

Junction for Waterloo
Latchmere Main Jtn
Latchmere SW Jtn

BATTERSEA

WLER to
Willesden
Junction (2)

Ludgate Jtn

Pig Hill
sidings

Clapham
Common

0.75

L&NWR
Falcon Lane
Goods

0.5

CLAPHAM
JUNCTION

Falcon Jtn

0.25

L&SWR
Carriage
sidings

CLAPHAM
COMMON

GWR New Wandsworth Goods

0

L&SWR
Windsor
line (4)

L&SWR main line (4)

NEW WANDSWORTH

LB&SCR main line (4)

THE BATTERSEA TANGLE
A Chronology of Railway Developments
Alan Postlethwaite

Comprehensive Map

The map (*opposite*) shows every pre-BR line, railway station and depot in Battersea although they did not all exist at the same time. Numbers of running lines are shown in brackets after the titles of key features. Yards and depots are shown with just one or two representative sidings. The three motive power depots (MPDs) show maximum development for steam including turntable dispositions.

Company Abbreviations

GWR	Great Western Railway
LB&SCR	London Brighton & South Coast Railway
LC&DR	London Chatham & Dover Railway
L&NWR	London & North Western Railway
L&SWR	London & South Western Railway
MR	Midland Railway
SE&CR	South Eastern & Chatham Railway
SER	South Eastern Railway
SR	Southern Railway
VS&PR	Victoria Station & Pimlico Railway
WEL&CPR	West End of London & Crystal Palace Railway (becoming part of the LB&SCR)
WLER	West London Extension Railway (joint GWR, LB&SCR, L&NWR, L&SWR)

Arrival of the 'South Western'

The London & Southampton Railway was built during 1834-40. The line was elevated on a viaduct across the fields of Battersea and terminated at Nine Elms. This was at the edge of the built-up area, some 300 yards from Vauxhall bridge and pleasure gardens. The concept was that passengers would complete their journey by river from Nine Elms pier into central London.

When Nine Elms terminus opened in 1838, the London & Southampton Railway was renamed L&SWR. Designed by Sir William Tite, the station building had a neo-classical frontage similar to Southampton Terminus. Some tracks crossed Nine Elms Lane (into Lambeth) to the wharf, the first MPD and the first works.

Also opening in 1838, the first station out of Nine Elms was Wandsworth. This was on the edge of Wandsworth Common but it was renamed Clapham Common shortly after opening. This was because Clapham was considered more genteel than Wandsworth and more likely to attract day-trippers. Clapham Common station closed in 1863 when Clapham Junction opened but the misnomer was perpetuated, the latter being in Battersea.

In 1841, Nine Elms works and MPD were rebuilt following a fire.

Below - Nine Elms station frontage.

National Railway Museum
Science & Society Picture Library

Above - *The 1838 shed at Nine Elms had a wooden truss roof. No cranes were added when it became goods-only in 1848.*

Below - *The late 1860s purpose-built goods shed at Nine Elms had a steel truss roof and jib cranes.*

THE BATTERSEA TANGLE

In 1846, the Richmond & West End Railway opened and was bought by the L&SWR in 1847. It joined the L&SWR main line where Clapham Junction is today. It was extended to reach Windsor in 1849.

During 1847-48, the L&SWR line through Battersea was widened from two to four tracks and the Metropolitan Extension opened to Waterloo with an intermediate station at Vauxhall. The purpose of the extension was to carry passengers nearer to the city centre rather than by the more cumbersome river boats. A further L&SWR extension to London Bridge never materialised.

In 1848, Nine Elms station became goods-only.

In 1849, a second (larger) MPD was opened south of Nine Elms Lane next to the goods station.

In 1854, a Royal Station opened at Nine Elms. It was re-sited c.1875 to the south of the main line, just north of the second works. It was last used briefly for troop trains of the Boer War (Ref. 8).

In 1861, Nine Elms Works and MPD started to move to a larger site south of the main line. The move was completed in 1869. A skew tunnel was built under the main line to connect the two sites, opening in 1916. In 1866, the L&SWR opened a spur from Ludgate junction to an end-on connection with the LC&DR at Lavender Hill junction. This was to allow Richmond trains to run to Ludgate Hill.

During the late 1860s, a purpose-built goods shed was built at Nine Elms on the site of the second MPD alongside the original shed.

In 1876, the third Nine Elms MPD was demolished to make way for widening of the lines to Waterloo. The replacement fourth MPD was a semi-roundhouse leading off two turntables, which lasted until c.1923.

In 1877, Queens Road station opened on the Windsor lines of the L&SWR. It carried the suffix 'Battersea' or 'Battersea Park' to differentiate it from a station of the same name in Peckham. Its name was changed to Queenstown Road in 1980.

In 1885, the fifth Nine Elms MPD was built to the south of the fourth. This was a straight shed with all 15 roads leading off the turntable. It became known as the Old Shed.

In 1891, Nine Elms carriage & wagon shops were transferred to Eastleigh. This allowed the locomotive works and MPD to expand.

In 1910, a New Shed of ten roads was built alongside the Old Shed and shared the same turntable.

Left - Queens Road station has two entrances. The main building is nicely preserved in L&SWR salmon pink. The booking office has been converted into a speciality coffee bar. The secondary entrance is semi-dilapidated under the railway bridge. It looks as though the bridge has been reinforced with additional beams and a tubular column. Long gone are the name, timetables and posters on the wall. 2012.

Left - *The tunnel connecting the fifth MPD with Nine Elms goods depot. This SR ancillary stop signal was on the south side. The RH tunnel was presumably for personnel. The curved double-slip would be a challenge to modellers. 1965.*

The New Shed and mighty SR coaling tower of Nine Elms MPD featuring a grimy 3MT tank No. 82039 1965. 53A Models of Hull Collection.

Arrival of the 'Brighton'

In 1855, the L&SWR withdrew from an agreement to allow LB&SCR traffic into Waterloo. (had the LB&SCR ever exercised that right?)

In 1858, the WEL&CPR opened a line to serve the Great Exhibition. The line burrowed under the L&SWR viaduct at Stewarts Lane and terminated at Pimlico where there was a wharf and pier. Pimlico station was by the south end of Chelsea road bridge.

Also in 1858, WEL&CPR opened stations at Stewarts Lane (closed in 1858) and at New Wandsworth (south of Clapham Junction). The latter closed to passengers in 1869 and the adjacent GWR coal depot closed in 1964.

Also in 1858, the WEL&CPR opened Battersea Park MPD just south of Pimlico station. It had three straight tracks (one a through road) with a turntable to the north of the shed. Three roundhouses followed. The original MPD closed to enable track realignment for the third roundhouse.

In 1859, the LB&SCR bought the WEL&CPR and the first roundhouse (circular) opened at Battersea Park MPD, west of the viaduct.

In 1860, the VS&PR opened a double-track line from the Brighton side of Victoria across Grosvenor Bridge to make an end-on connection with the LB&SCR at Stewarts Lane.

In 1860, Pimlico station closed and the first Battersea Park station opened at high level by the riverside. It closed in 1870.

In 1860, Pimlico station became goods-only and the second roundhouse (triangular) opened at Battersea Park MPD, east of the viaduct. The goods station was commonly known as Battersea Wharf.

Above - Next to Battersea Park station, a circular version of the LB&SCR coat of arms is cast into the ironwork of the railway bridge. The four quadrants are: the cross and sword of the City of London; the star and crescent of Portsmouth,; the two dolphins of Brighton; and three lions of the Cinque Ports (Hastings, Pevensey and Seaford). The date is 1865.

In 1867, Grosvenor Road station opened for ticket collection. It opened to LB&SCR passengers in 1870 until 1907.

In 1869, the L&NWR started a passenger service from the Brighton side of Victoria to Broad Street via the West London line. This was curtailed to Willesdon Junction in 1872.

In 1889, the third roundhouse (circular) opened at Battersea Park MPD, west of the viaduct. In the same year, the LB&SCR widened Grosvenor Bridge to give

Left - Battersea Park station frontage is wedged between the LB&SCR main line (L) and the South London line (R). 2012. Its Moorish style is reminiscent of buildings on the North London Line, Poplar branch.

Above - *This Thames panorama features three disparate styles of architecture: the graceful wrought iron Victorian arches of Grosvenor Bridge; the industrial 1930s brickwork of Battersea power station; and the glass-fronted modernity of luxury flats. The latter are built on the site of Battersea goods station. Heron and gannet now fish along this stretch of the river. 2012.*

Left - *In 1940, a bomb fell on the Up Local line at Battersea Park station. All services were restored within three days. Beyond the viaduct are the roofs of two former roundhouses of Battersea MPD. The third (triangular) roundhouse is less obvious to the right of the viaduct. The three roundhouses formed one great covered structure, turntable to turntable. The spur on the far left descended from the Up Main to the MPD headshunt at ground level. RCHS Spence Collection.*

Bluebell Credits - All illustrations are by the author unless otherwise stated. The photos by J J Smith were downloaded from the Bluebell Railway Museum Archive whose images can be perused on their website. As a Southern Region employee, John was able identify most inter-Regional trains and specials.

Top left - *The LB&SCR station building at Clapham Junction is in a super-suburban style of orange-red brick and Portland stone. The central door was to the parcels office. The main entrance today is on the middle floor from the forecourt (L). 2012.*

Bottom left - *The one remaining entrance to Wandsworth Road station is wedged between this corner and a locksmith. There is no trace of the LC&DR station beyond the bridge. 2012.*

Bottom right - *Although the style is LB&SCR, this signal bracket guards Stewarts Lane Junction from the LC&DR West London direction. An overhead ac gantry is visible on the South London viaduct and the scene is pre-cenotaph coaler at Stewarts Lane MPD. The photo is therefore pre-1934. J J Smith*

Above - At Longhedge class 5MT No. 44863 transfers from the West London line to the LC&DR line with a Rugby train to the Kent Coast. J J Smith, 1956.

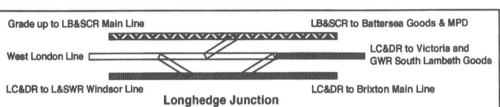

Grade up to LB&SCR Main Line	LB&SCR to Battersea Goods & MPD
West London Line	LC&DR to Victoria and GWR South Lambeth Goods
LC&DR to L&SWR Windsor Line	LC&DR to Brixton Main Line

Longhedge Junction

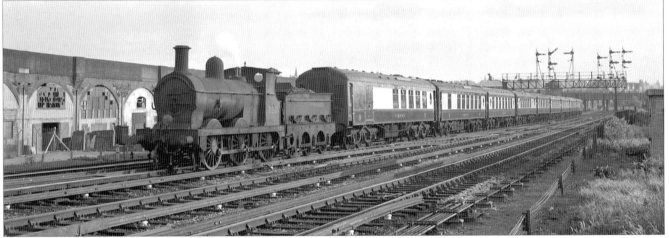

Above - Approaching Longhedge, Class O1 No. 31370 brings Bournemouth Belle empty stock from Clapham Junction to Stewarts Lane carriage sheds. The viaduct on the left is the LB&SCR main line rising from Pouparts Junction. J J Smith, 1959.

Left - At Longhedge, class M7 tank No. 30053 brings an LCGB special off the West London line towards Stewarts Lane. On the right, the LB&SCR line rises to Pouparts Junction. On the horizon is West London Junction overhead signal box. J J Smith, 1964.

Arrival of the 'Chatham'

In 1862, the LC&DR opened its main line from Brixton to Victoria, burrowing under the L&SWR at Stewarts Lane. It shared the LB&SCR's double-track line across Grosvenor Bridge until this was widened in 1866.

Also in 1862, the LC&DR opened its works, MPD and goods depot at Longhedge. The first MPD was a semi-roundhouse with 22 roads.

During 1862-63, the LC&DR built a line from Factory junction to connect with the WLER at Longhedge Junction. It remains to this day a key connection for cross-London freight traffic. In 1863, The LC&DR opened passenger stations at Stewarts Lane (closed in 1866) and at Wandsworth Road (closed in 1916).

The Chatham side of Victoria was also used by the GWR (to Southall), the Great Northern Railway (to Barnet) and the Midland Railway (to Hendon/ South Tottenham), the last two via the Widened Lines.

In 1866, the LC&DR built a spur from Longhedge Junction to connect end-on with the L&SWR at Lavender Hill Junction. It ran parallel with the West London line. In 1867, Grosvenor Road station opened to LC&DR passengers and closed in 1911.

In 1874, the MR opened a goods station at Wandsworth Road facing Stewarts Lane. Its traffic was routed via the Widened Lines, also via Barnes in BR days.

In 1875-76, Longhedge MPD was expanded to become a 40 road roundhouse. In 1880-81, the MPD was rebuilt as a 16 road through shed. Renamed Stewarts Lane, it was more commonly known as The Lane, Battersea or Longhedge.

In 1899, the LC&DR and SER merged operationally to become the SE&CR.

Above - A grand survivor is Grosvenor Road station building on the VS&PR. It served both the LC&DR and LB&SCR lines. The steel gate leads to the Chatham carriage sidings, 2012.

Below - LB&SCR 0-6-0 tank class E2 No. 32106 passes Wandsworth Road with a special train from Haywards Heath to Stewarts Lane. Has anyone lost a coach? J J Smith, 1953.

Right - LNER N1 No. 69445 passes Wandsworth Road with parcels from the Eastern Region to Battersea Wharf. J J Smith, 1953.

Left - Battersea home and Latchmere distant signals on a bracket of GWR design. Beyond is Battersea station and signal box. J J Smith

Right - Clapham Junction had 58 sidings. This view of the L&SWR sidings is taken from the great covered footbridge which served the LB&SCR and L&SWR station entrances. Mighty class H16 tank No. 30517 is relegated here to empty stock working. Beyond the curtained Maunsell restaurant car, the roofboard reads 'Newspaper Traffic Waterloo Ilfracombe'. 1958.

Clapham Junction is built on a brick viaduct except to the south-west (into Clapham cutting) and on the northern side where a steel bridge supports the west London platforms. The reason for the change from brick to steel is not obvious. A new booking hall (R) is at the north end of the great subway. There is another new booking hall at the south end. 2012.

Clapham Junction and the West London Line

Clapham Junction station opened in 1863, jointly owned by the L&SWR, LB&SCR and WLER. It became Europe's busiest station with seventeen platforms and some 2,500 trains per day. The name is a misnomer, perpetuated from an earlier station called Clapham Common (see L&SWR 1838). It should have been Battersea Junction .

In 1863, the WLER arrived from Willesden Junction with a station called Battersea (closed in 1940) and with four platforms at Clapham Junction. It made five key connections with other railways as follows:

A. With the L&SWR Windsor lines eastwards, used especially for freight to Nine Elms.

B. With the L&SWR Windsor lines westwards, used for passenger services terminating at Clapham Junction and transfers with the L&SWR main line.

C. With the LB&SCR at Falcon (later Clapham South) Junction. This was used for through-services between the south coast and the Midlands and North of England.

D. With the LB&SCR at Longhedge junction leading to the LB&SCR's Battersea goods station, MPD and Victoria.

E. With the LC&DR at Longhedge Junction, used by (a) GWR traffic to Victoria and South Lambeth goods depot and (b) cross-London traffic to Kent and (from 1929) to Hither Green marshalling yard.

In 1869, the L&NWR opened a goods depot at Falcon Lane (closed in 1968). Its entrance was from the southernmost West London platform of Clapham Junction.

Top - *Class E2 tank No. 32106 passes Latchmere Junction with a gas train to or from Pig Hill. J J Smith, 1956.*

Middle - *Class H tank No. 31321 at Latchmere with a Clapham Junction to Kensington local. The train included four ex-rail-motor coaches of the SE&CR. J J Smith, 1954.*

Bottom - *Class W tank No. 31912 passes Latchmere Junction with a Hither Green to Willesden freight. J J Smith, 1956.*

Top - *Clapham Junction 'B' signal box served the Brighton lines. The new box (L) opened in 1952 and closed in 1980. Behind the box were Pig Hill sidings where West London stock was stored and carriage gas was stored and produced (from oil). Its main use by the 1950s was for restaurant car cooking. See Ref. 6 for signalling details in the Battersea area. Thanks to Graham Floyd for this photo and advice.*

Middle - *An iconic feature of Clapham Junction was the 'A' signal box, one of several L&SWR overhead boxes between here and Waterloo. It opened in 1912 with the electro-pneumatic system, replaced by colour-light equipment in 1936. A steel roof was added during WW2 but was removed in 1965 following partial collapse of the corroded bridge. It closed in 1990. (Ref. 6.) J J Smith, 1930s.*

Bottom - *SE&CR class N Mogul No. 31826 arrives at Clapham Junction with a Hastings to Leicester train of Maunsell stock. The starting signals on the left are of the Sykes pattern. J J Smith, 1950.*

Note the long bridge from the L&SWR booking office near the Granada cinema. The SR closed this office and used the bridge for its Signalling School and Clerical Staff Training School. (SWIssue 11).

Arrival of the High Level Viaducts

In 1866, the VS&PR widened Grosvenor Bridge from two to seven tracks. The three western tracks were used by the LB&SCR. The other four ran to the Chatham side of Victoria, two of which were mixed gauge.

In 1866, the LC&DR opened its high-level viaduct to Grosvenor Bridge, avoiding the congested and steeply graded low-level route. In 1867, a new station opened on this viaduct called Battersea Park (...Road from 1877, closed in 1916).

In 1867, the LB&SCR opened its high-level 4-track viaduct from Pouparts junction to Grosvenor Bridge,

avoiding the congested and steeply graded low-level route. This was a continuation of its new main line from East Croydon via Streatham Common. The high-level York Road station opened at this time and was renamed Battersea Park in 1870.

Also in 1867, the LB&SCR's South London line opened from Peckham Rye to join the new main line at Battersea Park. At the same time, the LB&SCR's Wandsworth Road station opened on the South London line, adjacent to the LC&DR station of the same name. The companies must have been on good terms for one to bisect the depot of the other.

Above - A South London (ex-overhead ac stock) crosses the coal servicing roads of Stewarts Lane MPD. The turntable is behind the camera. The four tracks on the left are curving towards Stewarts Lane Junction. J J Smith, 1954.

Left - A cobbled lane burrows under the railway viaduct at Pouparts Junction. This is a magical tunnel, taking one back to the nineteenth century. Samuel Poupart was a local landowner who built some of the great housing estates hereabouts. The lane continues behind the camera to a ramped footbridge over the West London line and the Ludgate branch. 2012.

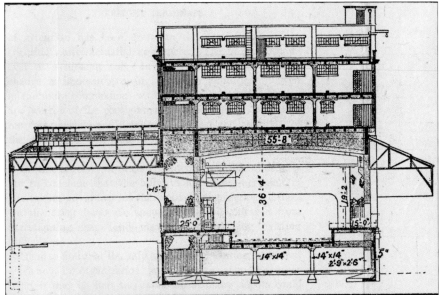

Above - *Early maps show two small good sheds at South Lambeth GWR depot. During 1911-13, the depot was rebuilt and enlarged to accommodate 350 wagons. The ultra-modern shed had a travelling jib crane. Reinforced concrete beams supported a multi-storey warehouse which was unique in South London. An extra storey was later added to the design. The depot closed c.1970. Ref. 13.*

Right - *Nothing remains of the L&SWR's Clapham Common station but this memorial has been erected nearby. It commemorates all those involved in the major accident of 1988 at this spot. The accident was caused by a loose wire in a colour-light signal.*

Below- *The LC&DR bridge at Queens Road is level with the house tops with their TV aerials and roof gardens. The two LB&SCR bridges are behind the camera. These three Windsor tracks were once busy with Nine Elms freight traffic. Platform 1 was added in 1877 but is now disused. The new skyscraper in the background is on the site of Nine Elms L&SWR wharf. 2012.*

THE BATTERSEA TANGLE

The 20th Century and Beyond

In 1908, the L&SWR opened a new works at Eastleigh and Nine Elms works closed in 1909.

From 1909, lines were electrified as follows:

A. During 1909-11, all LB&SCR principal running lines using the 6.6kV ac overhead system.

B. During 1915-16, all L&SWR principal running lines using the 630V dc outside third rail system which became standard for the Southern.

C. In 1925, the Chatham main line using the outside third.

D. During 1928-29, the LB&SCR overhead system was replaced by the outside third.

E. In 1993, the West London line to Kensington (outside 3rd).

In 1911, the SE&CR's Longhedge works closed (except for carriage and wagon repairs).

In 1915, GWR passenger services ceased between Victoria and Southall.

In 1923, the L&SWR, LB&SCR and SE&CR became principal parts of the Southern Railway grouping.

During 1929-33, the London Power Company built Battersea 'A' power station on the site of the reservoirs of the Southwark & Vauxhall Waterworks Company. It had a rail connection for delivery of heavy plant. The 'B' station opened during 1953-55. The 'A' station closed in 1975, followed by the 'B' station in 1983. The building is now a Heritage Site, Grade II* listed, awaiting a developer to give it a new use. The biggest brick building in Europe, it dominates the skyline of many a railway photograph, resembling an upturned billiard table. Another prominent feature nearby is a tall gas holder.

In 1934, following electrification of the Brighton main line, Battersea Park MPD closed and became a road transport depot. In the same year, Stewarts Lane MPD was rebuilt and enlarged to accommodate additional locomotives from Battersea Park. As part of this rebuild, Stewarts Lane acquired a cenotaph coaler and the turntable was moved to the west of the South London viaduct by the old works.

In 1937, the West London spur from the Waterloo direction was lifted. It was reinstated c.1990 to transfer Eurostar stock between Waterloo and North Pole train depot (now redundant) at Old Oak Common.

In 1940, there was major bomb damage to Nine Elms MPD, Stewarts Lane MPD and Battersea Park station (Ref. 11). Nine Elms Old Shed was so badly damaged that its front half was demolished and never rebuilt.

Nine Elms station building was also damaged by a WW2 bomb and was demolished in the 1960s.

In the 1950s, a new carriage shed was built adjacent to Stewarts Lane running shed. It had third rail electrification for servicing both EMUs and electric locomotives.

In 1957, Stewarts Lane goods depot was demolished.

During the 1960s, a new Traction Maintenance Depot was built on the site for both diesel and electric locomotives.

In 1963, Stewarts Lane MPD closed except for diesel locomotive servicing. The original shed was destroyed by fire in 1967.

In 1967, Nine Elms MPD closed. The site was redeveloped as the fruit and vegetable section of the new Covent Garden market, opening in 1974.

In 1968, Nine Elms goods depot closed. The site was redeveloped as the flower section of the new Covent Garden market, opening in 1974.

During 1990-92, a high-level viaduct was built to carry Eurostar services between the Chatham main line and the Windsor line to Waterloo (not shown on the comprehensive map). It became redundant in 2007 when the new Eurostar terminus opened at St Pancras.

In 2008, the Virgin Birmingham-Brighton service was withdrawn and replaced by a Parliamentary service of one train per weekday in each direction between Wandsworth Road and Kensington Olympia. Running this useless service is apparently more economic than seeking to repeal legislation for the Birmingham-Brighton service.

Passenger services between Clapham Junction and Stratford via the West London and North London lines are run these days by London Overground. They introduced a new service in 2012 between Clapham Junction and Highbury & Islington via the South London and East London lines.

There are plans to extend the Northern Line tube to Battersea as part of the power station redevelopment. It would branch from the reversing loop of the Charing Cross line at Stockwell with an intermediate station at Nine Elms.

References

1. Dendy Marshall, CF, revised by Kidner, RW, *History of the Southern Railway*, Ian Allan, 1963.

2. The Loco Shed Index (website).

3. White, HP, *A Regional History of the Railways of Great Britain Volume 3 Greater London*, David & Charles, 1963.

4. Bolger, Paul, *BR Motive Power Depots SR*, Ian Allan, 1983.

5. Course, Edwin, *The Foreign Goods Depots of South London*, Railway Magazine, November 1960.

6. Adlington, Mark, *Clapham Junction 'B' Signal Box*, website.

7. Kent Rail website - Stewarts Lane.

8. Borley, HV, Chronology of London's Railways.

9. Railway Clearing House, Railway Junction Diagram of Clapham Junction, Stewarts Lane, Lavender Hill and Longhedge, 1912 & 1914 (website).

10. Leigh, Chris, *The Aerofilms Book of Britain's Railways from the Air*, Ian Allan, 1987.

11. The Southern Way Special Issue No. 5, *Wartime Southern Part 2*, Noodle Books, 2010.

12. http://www.flickr.com/photos/blue-diesels/6021600534/in/photostream/

13. Lamb, David R, *Modern Railway Operation*, Pitman's Transport Library, 1941.

14. The Signal Box Photo Gallery website.

15. Mitchell, Vic & Smith, Keith, six books of the Middleton Press on the following lines: *Waterloo to Windsor; Waterloo to Woking; Victoria to Bromley South; Victoria to East Croydon; the South London Line; the West London Line.*

SOUTHERN

MIXED TRAFFIC LOCOMOTIVES

"Merchant Navy" Class

Naming Ceremony

OF

"SHAW SAVILL"

AT

VICTORIA STATION

Thursday, 30th July, 1942

BY

LORD ESSENDON

Chairman

Shaw Savill & Albion Company, Limited.

accompanied by Southern Railway Deputy Chairman, Col. Eric Gore-Browne D.S.O.,
and General Manager, Mr. E. J. Missenden

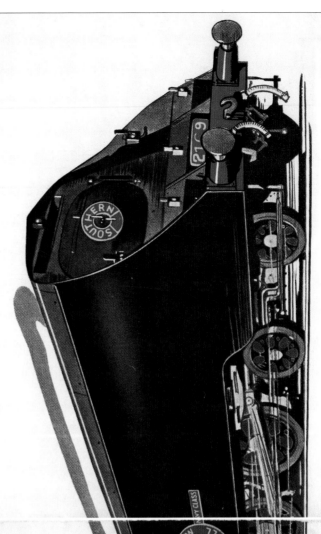

SHAW SAVILL LINES

The Shaw Savill Line, founded in 1858, has earned its high reputation in the New Zealand trade by keeping abreast—and even ahead—of the technical development demanded by changing conditions and by a constant policy of caring for the comfort and welfare of its passengers.

In pursuance of this policy Southampton has, for many years, been used as the port of embarkation and disembarkation for passengers and for the discharge of cargo, the facilities for which the Southern Railway has done so much to develop.

The latest addition to the fleet, the quadruple screw motor vessel "DOMINION MONARCH," of 27,155 tons, is the largest and most powerful motor vessel trading to South Africa, Australia and New Zealand, and is now, as she was in the days of peace, an important link in Empire communications.

The Shaw Savill vessels have always been Empire food carriers—it was, in fact, the Shaw Savill & Albion vessel "DUNEDIN," in 1882, that brought the first cargo of frozen meat from New Zealand to England—and the immense capacity of the present-day vessels of the Line is a vital asset to the Country now.

The flag is of particular interest, as it was the National Flag of New Zealand chosen by the Maori chiefs in 1834, and was adopted by Shaw Savill & Albion Company in 1858, it having ceased to be the National flag when New Zealand came under British Sovereignty.

The other engines of this class will be named as under, each bearing a replica of the House Flag of the Shipping Line concerned. They have been chosen by reason of their association with Southampton Docks, which are owned and managed by the Southern Railway. No. 1 "Channel Packet," No. 2 "Union Castle," No. 3 "Royal Mail," No. 4 "Cunard White Star," No. 5 "Canadian Pacific," No. 6 "P. & O.," No. 7 "Aberdeen & Commonwealth," are already in service.

Orient
Blue Star

The significance of including the names allocated to Nos 21C8 and 21C10 without further reference is unclear.

All classes of Engines are being painted black as a wartime measure.

NAMING CEREMONY 'SHAW SAVILL', 30 JULY 1942

Christopher Purdie

A fascinating piece of Southern Railway ephemera has recently come to light in the shape of a publicity leaflet which was issued to dignitaries and guests who attended the naming ceremony of Merchant Navy 'Pacific' 21C9 *Shaw Savill* at Victoria Station on 30 July 1942.

The leaflet probably serves to sustain rather than resolve the debate over the Southern Railway's introduction of Oliver Bulleid's radical new design during wartime. On the one hand, title of the leaflet confirms that the Southern Railway actively promoted the initial members of the class as "Mixed Traffic Locomotives" at this time, having applied the classification to enable the locomotives to be built during wartime. On the other hand, one cannot help but wonder how seriously the Southern sought to conceal its true intentions because the striking stylised illustration of 21C9, running 'light engine' at speed with a trailing exhaust, fully evokes the pre-war imagery of the streamlined express passenger locomotive. The one concession to the sombre reality of the wartime railway is the locomotive's austere black livery.

Seventy years on, it seems remarkable that the Southern Railway's publicity machine was so active during wartime and one wonders to what extent such activities carried government sanction in the interests of promoting the morale of the nation. Several of the naming ceremonies were reported in the national press and at least one, for 21C1 *Channel Packet* at Eastleigh on 10 March 1941, was filmed for the newsreels.

The decision of the Southern Railway to quietly abandon its original intention to name the new locomotives after Allied victories in the war seems particularly prudent, given the limited extent of military success in the early stages of the war. Even by the time of 21C9's naming in July 1942, and despite the strengthening of Britain's longer term strategic fortunes by the entry of the United States into the war, recent months had seen a string of failures, including the loss of Singapore in the Far East and the Axis victories at Gazala and Tobruk in the Western Desert.

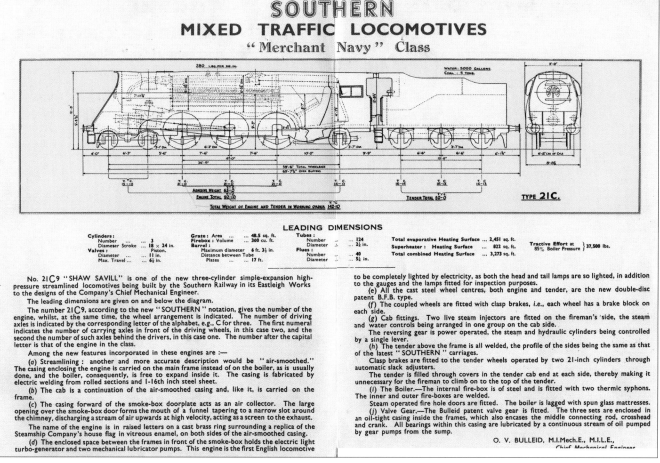

SOUTHERN
MIXED TRAFFIC LOCOMOTIVES
"Merchant Navy" Class

TYPE 21C.

LEADING DIMENSIONS

Cylinders:		Grate: Area ... ... 48.5 sq. ft.	Tubes:		Total evaporative Heating Surface ... 2,451 sq. ft.	
Number 3		Firebox : Volume ... 300 cu. ft.	Number 124		Superheater : Heating Surface ... 822 sq. ft.	Tractive Effort at 85% Boiler Pressure } 37,500 lbs.
Diameter Stroke ... 18 x 24 in.		Barrel :	Diameter ... 2¼ in.		Total combined Heating Surface ... 3,273 sq. ft.	
Valves :	Piston.	Maximum diameter 6 ft. 3½ in.	Flues :			
Diameter ... ... 11 in.		Distance between Tube	Number 40			
Max. Travel ... ... 6¼ in.		Plates ... ... 17 ft.	Diameter ... ... 5¼ in.			

No. 21C9 "SHAW SAVILL" is one of the new three-cylinder simple-expansion high-pressure streamlined locomotives being built by the Southern Railway in its Eastleigh Works to the designs of the Company's Chief Mechanical Engineer.

The leading dimensions are given on and below the diagram.

The number 21C9, according to the new "SOUTHERN" notation, gives the number of the engine, whilst, at the same time, the wheel arrangement is indicated. The number of driving axles is indicated by the corresponding letter of the alphabet, e.g., C for three. The first numeral indicates the number of carrying axles in front of the driving wheels, in this case two, and the second number of such axles behind the drivers, in this case one. The number after the capital letter is that of the engine in the class.

Among the new features incorporated in these engines are :—

(a) Streamlining : another and more accurate description would be "air-smoothed." The casing enclosing the engine is carried on the main frame instead of on the boiler, as is usually done, and the boiler, consequently, is free to expand inside it. The casing is fabricated by electric welding from rolled sections and 1-16th inch steel sheet.

(b) The cab is a continuation of the air-smoothed casing and, like it, is carried on the frame.

(c) The casing forward of the smoke-box doorplate acts as an air collector. The large opening over the smoke-box door forms the mouth of a funnel tapering to a narrow slot around the chimney, discharging a stream of air upwards at high velocity, acting as a screen to the exhaust.

The name of the engine is in raised letters on a cast brass ring surrounding a replica of the Steamship Company's house flag in vitreous enamel, on both sides of the air-smoothed casing.

(d) The enclosed space between the frames in front of the smoke-box holds the electric light turbo-generator and two mechanical lubricator pumps. This engine is the first English locomotive

to be completely lighted by electricity, as both the head and tail lamps are so lighted, in addition to the gauges and the lamps fitted for inspection purposes.

(e) All the cast steel wheel centres, both engine and tender, are the new double-disc patent B.F.B. type.

(f) The coupled wheels are fitted with clasp brakes, i.e., each wheel has a brake block on each side.

(g) Cab fittings. Two live steam injectors are fitted on the fireman's side, the steam and water controls being arranged in one group on the cab side.

The reversing gear is power operated, the steam and hydraulic cylinders being controlled by a single lever.

(h) The tender above the frame is all welded, the profile of the sides being the same as that of the latest "SOUTHERN" carriages.

Clasp brakes are fitted to the tender wheels operated by two 21-inch cylinders through automatic slack adjusters.

The tender is filled through covers in the tender cab end at each side, thereby making it unnecessary for the fireman to climb on to the top of the tender.

(i) The Boiler.—The internal fire-box is of steel and is fitted with two thermic syphons. The inner and outer fire-boxes are welded.

Steam operated fire hole doors are fitted. The boiler is lagged with spun glass mattresses.

(j) Valve Gear.—The Bulleid patent valve gear is fitted. The three sets are enclosed in an oil-tight casing inside the frames, which also encases the middle connecting rod, crosshead and crank. All bearings within this casing are lubricated by a continuous stream of oil pumped by gear pumps from the sump.

O. V. BULLEID, M.I.Mech.E., M.I.L.E.,
Chief Mechanical Engineer

The naming of the locomotives after merchant shipping companies which had called at Southampton Docks in peacetime was an astute decision which was likely to resonate with the government and the public alike because of the Merchant Navy's heavy involvement in the war effort, not least in sustaining the vital Atlantic convoys against the ever-present threat of U-boats. The true scale of this contribution and its ultimate price, the loss of more than 32,000 merchant seamen, would only emerge after the war.

The Shaw Savill Line's ships certainly fulfilled the leaflet's claim to be "a vital asset to the Country now". Taken up by the government at the outbreak of war, several ships in the company's inventory served as troop and supply ships, whilst others were converted into Armed Merchant Cruisers for convoy escort duty and blockade patrol ships. Sadly, losses were suffered throughout the war and, just two weeks after the Shaw Savill Line was honoured at Victoria, three of its ships, the *Empire Hope*, *Wairangi* and *Waimarama* were lost to enemy action in the Mediterranean during 'Operation Pedestal', the Royal Navy's successful but costly attempt to run a heavily protected convoy of merchant ships past Axis bombers, E-boats, U-boats and minefields to relieve the besieged island of Malta.

In the post-war years, ships of the Shaw Savill Line continued to serve predominantly New Zealand ports and were particularly active in carrying migrant passengers. The final ships to fly the company's flag sailed in 1985, by which time trade had declined and its operations had gradually been subsumed within those of its owning group. By this time, 21C9 (later 35009) *Shaw Savill* had already ceased to fly the company's flag on the railway, having been withdrawn in July 1964. Happily, *Shaw Savill* survived at Barry and, albeit currently in a dismantled state at Bury, the locomotive will hopefully one day return to steam to provide future generations with a fitting memorial to the former shipping line and its contribution to the Allied war effort.

Associated paperwork from the Michael Brooks collection.

Left - *A similar brochure had been produced for the naming of No 21C6 in the previous month whilst a number of similar brochures reference the naming of other members of the class.*

Right - *Just over a decade later, in service at Salisbury with a down passenger working, 28 July 1955.*

Tony Molyneaux

'SHAW SAVILL'

Permanent Way Notes by Graham Hatton

RAIL FAILURES and DETECTION PROCEDURES

Introduction

This article is very much an overview of the development of Ultrasonics as used extensively in the rail industry.

The use of ultrasonic sound waves, emitted from a special probe into a suitable material (in this case, a steel rail), and reflected off a distant edge back to the probe before being electronically analysed, is not new technology and is not unique to the railways. Many industries find ultrasonic analysis an excellent way to see what is happening within a non-transparent material or body.

The process is adaptable to look for very specific faults within a body which may or may not have a hard composition. And its uses range from analysing railway axles and aircraft parts to monitoring unborn babies. In each case the probe and reflected signal have been 'honed' with time to detect a specific fault or shape within an object. Ultrasonic waves can be reflected from within the body to maximise the ability to see around 'blind' areas and it closely follows the principles of light reflection within prisms as taught in science lessons at school.

However I am confining this article to how ultrasonics have developed in the Permanent Way world, giving a few examples of the sort of failures (which are often invisible to the naked eye) that it is capable of detecting when used by a trained operator. That is until they cause a visible failure which may have the potential to be catastrophic in nature, though with advancing technology the number of previously undetected failures is now very small.

The modern equipment also allows you to size failures. This is especially useful to detect the size of a crack and hence the corrective action required, or in some materials where crack propagation is slower (such as high manganese steel) to monitor the growth of a crack over a period of time.

The equipment in use is now very advanced and can be mounted under a suitable specialised rail vehicle or propelled in a hand-powered unit which is similar in basic principle to that illustrated below, but modern equipment had to start somewhere in its development and the illustrations used date largely from around 1960 to the mid-1970s.

Photo 1 - opposite

This illustration shows the early basic equipment which at this time for this particular application used an audio method for listening to the reflected wave.

It shows ultrasonic ganger (the word operator appears to have come later) E. Barkleit being instructed in the use of an Audigage Rail Flaw Detector by J. Banks of the CCE Department. The lookout with traditional furled flags is P. Thomas. This is dated 1964, but the specific location is only known to be somewhere on the Southern system.

The set up here is being used to look for cracks around fishplate holes.

The rail is 'worked or flexed' by the action of loaded wheels passing along it which induces stress in the rail. Such stresses at the rail ends are prone to develop fatigue cracking around any imperfection, which in this area is commonly any tiny fault around the drilled fishplate holes, though there are other causes of rail end failures. In the case of rail ends the common fracture from a fishbolt hole tends to be at 45 degrees to the horizontal and can be in any one of the four diagonal directions emanating from any bolt hole.

The ultrasonic wave is created electrically and converted into mechanical oscillation by a crystal. Various angles of probes containing the crystal are used. The ultrasonic detector will measure the time interval between an ultrasonic wave entering the rail and reflecting harmlessly off the rail foot back to a receiver. If there is a crack emanating from a bolt hole between the rail top and bottom the crack reflects the wave back to the probe receiver and the time interval between entry and exit of the wave in the rail will be considerably less. An ultrasonic wave will not pass across a crack but will be reflected.

The angle of the probe used here was actually 40 degrees as this was found to match any crack, lying at roughly 90 degrees to it. Of course this only detects cracks in one diagonal (slanted) plane. To see the other diagonal plane (90 degrees to the first), the ultrasonic probe being slowly slid along the rail surface over the fishbolt area was reversed and 'looked' the other way. The process evolved to use other angles of probes to 'see around' bolt holes whilst avoiding the problems of reflections from the second hole and the rail ends. A second probe at 0 degrees and mounted in the rail carrier looked straight down for any horizontal cracking under the rail head which would be difficult to see but is a fairly common failure at rail ends. Because of the two probe angles, until recently this was known as 040 testing, because of the 0+40 degree probes.

A 'coupling' medium has to be used between the probe and the rail, and the rail industry is lucky that soapy water was found to work well for this and is probably contained in the tin. Ultrasonic waves will not effectively pass across even a very small air gap.

Such cracks around bolt holes were known as 'star cracks' due to their angles of normal failure from the bolt hole. They can start from a very small dent in a rail hole and have an initial length leading to failure of little more than 1mm, so detection has to be accurate.

The fear of all Permanent Way men is the end, or first, bolt hole will have a star crack failure which can lead to a triangular section of rail about 5inches long being literally bounced out of a rail end (and seldom found), such a failure then leading to a very severe hammer blow across the now very considerable rail head gap. This can ultimately result in the rail end breaking up, with the obvious concern that this could be catastrophic with high train speeds.

When detected at the rail end star crack failures demand immediate attention. A complete failure of a rail end with subsequent break out of a triangular section can happen within days. The modern railway as stated is very well equipped to detect such failures but also modern track eliminates bolt holes as far as possible, using continuous welded rail and welded switches and crossings.

Nothing should ever be put in a fishplate hole except an appropriate bolt. The use of bars to turn rails is prohibited as a hexagonal bar, put in a bolt hole, is the starting point for many such cracks resulting from the dent caused by levering forces on the angular edges of such a bar (to say nothing of the dangers caused to the operative should the rail 'flip' over, as the bar can become a lethal weapon.)

Photo 2 - below

This is a slightly earlier view and shows a trained operator checking the fishbolt area on the rail end. The ganger stands ready to remove the fishplate for a visual inspection should an adverse signal be detected.

Audigage equipment used a variation in tone in the earphones to tell the operator what the equipment was looking at. This was developed into a dial on the handle to view the same information.

Later equipment by Krautkramer made use of transistors and consisted of an oscilloscope with a visual screen showing the reflected wave. The oscilloscope would be calibrated at the start of each day against samples carried or available with known faults. Such calibration would allow the reflected signal to be maximised on the screen and have a known size. Across the oscilloscope screen 'gates' or 'lines' could be created electronically, such that a sudden spike in the signal on the screen, as found when the probe detected a crack, would cause an audible alarm to alert the operator to any fault, should he not have noticed it on the screen.

This equipment was used for rail end detection, but similar equipment with a different probe angle of 70 degrees, designed to look for the fault known as a Tache

Photo 3.

Ovale, and 0 degree or vertical fixed probes to look for other near horizontal cracks, was known till fairly recently, as 070 equipment and used for testing the full rail, outside the fishplate limits. Again development had found these angles to be best suited to this situation.

In the full rail the common failures include the fault known as a 'Tache Ovale'. These grow within the rail head (or table) and are often seen as a black depression initially, developing into a V or kidney shaped failure. They can grow to an alarming size within the head before causing a rail failure and have several triggers to start them. They occur in one rail only.

They are often confused with railburns or wheelburns caused by a wheel turning or slipping whilst stationary or nearly stationary. The huge loads and very small contact area will create immense heat in a short period and locally melt the rail head. Cracking and failures from these can be similar to Tache Ovales but wheelburns are usually in both rails as the whole wheel axle slips. They can of course be imported to other sites and cause problems later by changing rails.

Wheelburns are common on gradients and places where trains start. In steam days, locos often slipped on wet rails and with lighter axle loading/ larger diameter wheels caused less damage. The advent of electric stock with small wheels, some of which had axle hung motors adding to the

weight, caused the whole problem of wheelburns to be increased. If serious and not weld-repaired these could easily lead to further rail failures. Modern electric and diesel stock has sophisticated equipment to prevent wheels slipping, but early Southern electric units of course relied on the driver's skill to 'ease off' when forward motion was not forthcoming! There are examples of extreme wheelburns where the wheel has virtually melted the rail from the head through to the foot when a train has not moved at all under power to the wheels, or the motor has malfunctioned, but even small wheelburns create real dents from which cracks can develop by the increased hammer-blow effect. Such cracks being below a depressed surface are even more difficult to test ultrasonically as the probe cannot easily be 'coupled' to the rail surface as it is irregular and depressed. The reverse is of course familiar to many as the 'flat' on a wheel where rotation has stopped and the wheel slides along the rail causing similar very high friction burns and ultimately wheel damage.

Some faults found in rails can actually develop in the wheel tyre as well, and of course axles are also subject to ultrasonic testing as failures of these, such as the failure of a steam loco driving wheel axle on Merchant Navy No. 35020 *Bibby Line* passing at 70mph through Crewkerne station in 1953, can be equally as catastrophic.

Over time all sorts of tests have been evolved to

29

look for various rail faults. Because of the way the process works, though, in general different faults need different processes to detect them. It is not a 'one size fits all' situation in ultrasonic detection.

Photo 3 - page 29.

In this case a dubious signal has been detected, the fishplate has been removed and the crack is being visually inspected using a hand held mirror. A piece of highly polished plate in a carrying case was commonly used as a mirror to avoid breakage problems. Note that at this stage much of the equipment was carried in a back pack or pushed into a large pocket.

Once detected, the size and angle was critical. Over time very precise action plans were developed, but obviously before the days of mobile phones, urgent action would be via the use of flags and detonators as laid down in the Rule Book in extreme cases, or 'hot footing' it to the nearest signal box or lineside phone to summon help or reduce train speeds.

The size was critical as the crack length also determined if a speed restriction would be imposed, particularly if the crack extended from the bolt hole up into

the rail head and was therefore far more likely to cause a rail end failure. Reflected waves are complex in fishplate areas and the operator would be trained to avoid spurious signals and shadow areas. Less well known, but an area which caused further failure potential, was the Southern's love of drilling two small bond holes between the fishplate holes of adjacent rails; a copper bond was fixed between them to maintain electrical continuity of the return DC traction current. This practice added to the complexity of the reflected ultrasonic waves and was eventually discontinued.

Photo 4 - above.

Inevitably the process gradually became mechanised to a degree. The testing of the full rail as opposed to just the rail end was so extensive that the obvious answer was to mount the equipment on a rail vehicle, in this case an adapted trolley. In this undated view the equipment has an oscilloscope mounted top centre. The probes are mounted to run along the rail and are fed with a steady small stream of soapy water as the coupling medium.

On the right in the picture, on the trolley, there is a small generator to power the equipment, probably via a battery to give voltage stabilisation.

It is assumed that at this stage the equipment was pushed and the operator may have sat in the back of the trolley to view the oscilloscope screen. The probe equipment and fluid supply can be seen in front of the trolley wheel on the left.

Over time it was found easier to mount the oscilloscope and small water supply on a 'walking stick' which could be used to look at one rail at a time in places of reasonable visibility between trains, being removed and replaced for their passage simply by lifting on and off the rail.

Another development was equipment mounted in a purpose-built train which travelled around the system on a regular basis, initially as a back up to the hand propelled equipment. Because the train did not normally stop, faults were logged and 'verified' by operators despatched to site accordingly. Probes were eventually contained in hard wearing fluid filled flexible globes with further fluid liberally spread under the globe on the rail head, but inevitably some areas were missed and required to be followed up. These train-mounted probes were capable of being lifted, for instance around switches and crossings and level crossings to avoid them being torn to pieces on sharper rail and road surfaces.

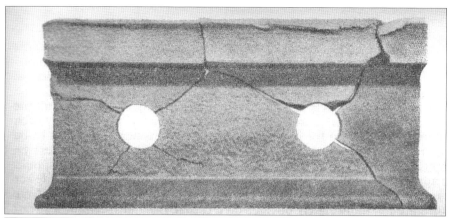

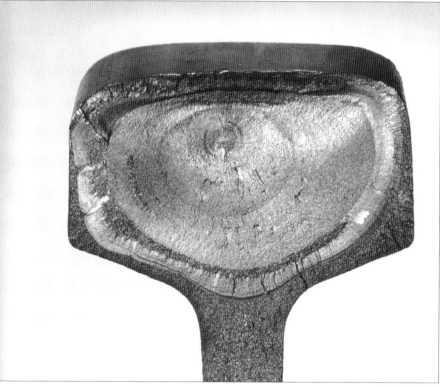

Photo 5 - this page top.

Looking now at the faults being detected, this more recent view shows an extreme 'star crack' failure reassembled. The rail end here has broken up and the wheel has bounced across the very significant gap that existed in the rail head and resulted in a hammer blow effect to the remaining rail end. This can happen quickly after the initial crack has formed.

Star cracks are normally formed in only one plane.

Photo 6 - this page bottom.

This is a good picture of an unusually large fault of a classic Tache Ovale failure. This fault often starts with a tiny pressurised bubble of hydrogen gas in the rail head trapped during the rail's molten forming and rolling stages. The centre of the original inclusion can be clearly seen, and around this have grown rings, very much in the style of growth rings in trees. As the fault develops there is a loss of strength, and in this case the crack actually covered the rail head and broke out on the surface with a complete crack through the rail through a general loss of solid section.

It was not unusual in earlier days for such failures to have hung on by a small head area before the wheel forces broke the rail. This could be seen after the failure as the old crack was weathered and blacker, the final break being light grey.

Earlier rails, like wine, have good and bad years, and there have been specific years in which rolled rails have been subject to above average problems. 1965 rail, commonly installed in the extensive relaying of the Southampton main line prior to third rail electrification of this route, suffered particularly from this problem of Tache Ovales, though there are other years and other locations. Again, rail technology was improved and present-day rail suffers less from this fault.

Photo 7 - opposite top.

Another fault which occurs principally on Bullhead rail is rail gall.

This is the significant wearing of the rail foot in the cast iron chair. In the case viewed here from the underside of the rail, a rail break has occurred from the end of a portion of gall on the left, the chair housing having also dug into the side of the rail. The amount of allowable rail gall in a rail is limited. It often occurs in wet areas, such as a sea pier where sea air and attrition wear away the rail, for example Ryde Pier IOW. But equally, wet tunnels have the same effect and this failure occurred in Grove Tunnel, Tunbridge Wells.

As ultrasonic equipment developed and the use of a fully calibrated screen on an oscilloscope became available, instead of just an audible signal, it became possible to measure accurately the depth of the rail by the displayed signal on a calibrated screen and therefore the slightly smaller depth of the area where rail gall occurred. The difference could then be quoted and monitored until a set level was reached when the rail would be changed. This is actually a particularly difficult fault to see unless the rail is removed.

Photo 8 - opposite bottom.

Ultrasonics is not the only system (apart from visual examination) to detect faults.

Magnetic particle detection of a weld was developed to emphasise the fault using electromagnetic waves and iron filings.

The changes in the magnetic waves around a crack attract the iron filings emphasising the crack. This is seldom used nowadays; the similar dye penetrant system has replaced it for highlighting these cracks.

This uses a number of chemicals in spray tins. A penetrating oil with a red dye is sprayed on the cleaned area to be tested and allowed to surface dry. Then a developer is sprayed on, a bit like chalk, which draws out of the crack any damp red penetrant which cannot dry so easily, thus showing the position of the crack clearly as a red on white line on the rail. This system is still used extensively when testing weld repaired crossings to check that all old cracks have been removed before new layers of weld repair material are added to build the crossing up to its original shape.

In the days when Bishops Waltham had a railway - now it has a roundabout on the same site. (There is just no comparison.) The twice / thrice weekly goods from Botley servicied the terminus in the early 1960s. This working had continued for almost 30 years after passenger closure from 31 December 1932 until all working ceased from 27 April 1962.

WEST COUNTRY JOURNEY

In August 1962 Jeffery Grayer took his annual holiday in the West Country and made timely visits to both Barnstaple Junction and Wadebridge sheds just in time to capture some veteran steam in their twilight hours.

This page - One of the attractions of Barnstaple shed were the M7 tanks which had been a feature of 72E for a good many years. By 1962 their days here were numbered and in this view a brace of them, 30025 based at Exmouth Junction at this time and 30254 based locally, can be seen awaiting their next call of duty.

Opposite page - No. 30251, another 72E locomotive, waits by the coaling stage whilst a couple of Maunsell Moguls can be seen in the distance. The last M7 based here, No. 30670, departed in January 1963 a few months after these scenes were taken.

Opposite page - *More modern types were beginning to infiltrate by this time as witnessed by the presence of an Ivatt tank, of which eight were based here in 1962, alongside original Bulleid Pacific No. 34015 "Exmouth". This 'West Country' was based at Exmouth Junction and often worked up to Barnstaple and Ilfracombe on long distance and local passenger services.*

Above - *A positive plethora of steam glimpsed from the carriage window of a departing Exeter train, also of course steam hauled. Two M7s are on view together with a Maunsell Mogul, an Ivatt and a WC.*

Right - *On 22 August 1962 Wadebridge shed played host to N Mogul No. 31835, whilst inside lurked two of the newly arrived Pannier Tanks plus the sole remaining 0298 Beattie Well Tank, which had finished regular work just the day before my visit but was retained here to work an LCGB enthusiasts special to Wenfordbridge on the 8 September.*

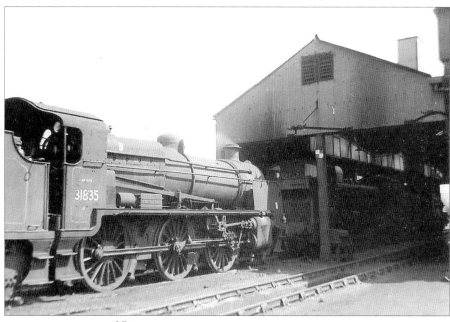

Opposite top - *The sole surviving Beattie tank at Wadebridge at the time of my visit, No. 30587, seen inside the shed with two of the trio of Pannier Tanks, Nos. 1369 and 1367, recently drafted in as replacements from the Weymouth Quay line.*

Opposite bottom - *The third replacement was No. 1368 seen here outside the Goods Shed: one of the few surviving buildings at Wadebridge today. These replacements had a relatively short life in this Cornish outpost, lasting only until 1964 when diesels took over their primary duty, which was handling clay traffic on the Wenfordbridge line.*

Above - *Exmouth Junction based N Mogul No. 31842 runs light engine through the station with the shed's large water tank and the station's concrete running in board prominent in the background.*

Right - *The signalman at Padstow leans from the window of his cabin whilst a Maunsell Mogul runs round.*

Halcyon Days: Above - Southern E6X No 2407.
Below - E5 No. LBSCR 400 amongst the opposition, including an 'Ilfracombe Goods' at Strawberry Hill.
Later years - Lost in wraiths of steam an unidentified E4 arrives in Bognor Regis to head for the MPD. The absence of a smoke box number plate suggests pre-1948 but makes identification impossible. The advance starter by the signal box, electric multiple unit sidings and approach roads to the terminus in the centre of the picture and all but fade into the mist of steam.

THE FINAL YEARS OF THE 'BRIGHTON RADIALS'

Bill Allen

Local passenger, freights, shunting and empty stock workings were, in the 1950s often the preserve of Victorian and Edwardian tank engines. The Southern region was no different from the other parts of British Railways in this pre-diesel era. One series of classes that came into this category were the 0-6-2Ts designed by Robert Billinton for the LBSCR and built at Brighton. Whether around the lines of their pre-grouping origin or farther afield at such places as Eastleigh, Basingstoke, Nine Elms or Tonbridge, E3s, E4s, E5s and E6s were usefully employed for many years. The photographs by Ron & Bill Allen in this brief article illustrate the "Radials" in diverse locations. We missed photographing E5s and the re-boilered E4Xs, E5Xs and E6Xs but certainly the E5s and E5Xs made visits to our home at Bognor. E3s were also more elusive and eluded the camera.

Historically the genesis of the locomotives is interesting. They bridge the succession between Stroudley and Billinton as CME of the LBSCR. The first radial No 158 *West Brighton* was designed by Stroudley, incorporating aspects of his enlarged E1 0-6-0T *Barcelona*. Stroudley died before the locomotive was completed and Billinton completed the task. It was not a complete success (often the fate of prototypes); it spent its working life on the south coast and was condemned and scrapped in 1934. Billinton had seen enough in this much more powerful tank engine than the then universal E1; so he perpetuated the design as the E3, entering service between 1894 and 1895. Initially they found employment on suburban services but were soon relegated to goods and shunting where they remained employed for over a half century. Modified with new boilers and extended smokeboxes, they all entered BR service in 1948 and were re-numbered 32165-170 and 32453-62. From being scattered over the system they became concentrated at Norwood Junction and Bricklayers Arms with one or two at Brighton, Tonbridge and Tunbridge Wells. The death knell was diesel shunters and the final three survived at Norwood until 1959 with creditable final mileages of over one million miles each.

After this experience and the realisation that an increase in driving-wheel size might make a more suitable passenger tank, Billinton produced the "Large Radial" E4. The driving-wheel diameter increased from 4' 6" to 5' and as D.L Bradley describes in 'Locomotives of the LBSCR Part 3', "In traffic they proved so generally useful for both goods and passenger duties that they became a stock design

to which a total of 75 were built at Brighton Works." Elegant and well-liked by their crews they still had severe limitations on semi-fast passenger trains. The increase in wheel size was not a recipe for a free-running locomotive – unfortunately, a cramped valve-chest design made steam flow poor and at over 40mph the engine "choked" due to an inability to exhaust the steam quickly enough. So, for their lifetime, branch passenger and freight duties were their metier – and they certainly were excellent at these tasks. Four were rebuilt as E4X using I2 boilers. The rest entered BR service – most receiving BR black lined secondary livery. By 1962 only four remained 32468/74/9 and 32503

and the last survivor 32479 was withdrawn from Newhaven in June 1963. However that was not the end of the E4s – 32473 had already, in October 1962, been sold to the Bluebell Railway and survives, having worn a variety of liveries over recent years, doing sterling service and not threatening her "speed limit" of 40mph on this restricted speed limit preserved railway. She remains a delightful reminder of this group of classes and the Victorian/ Edwardian age she came from.

Billinton's next design, the E5 appeared in 1902, and here continued his quest for a free-running and - steaming mixed traffic tank engine. The E5s had a bigger boiler, 5'6" drivers and a distinctive squat, tapered, chimney that was retained throughout their lives. Billinton never quite came to terms with the front end problem but the E5s were speedy machines, well capable of secondary passenger work.

The E5s had good acceleration which enhanced their use on intermediate services with lots of station stops. Post-war arrival of LMS and then Standard 2-6-4Ts eliminated their passenger work, so they found use in freight and shunting for which they were not perhaps as suitable as

their predecessors. Worn out, they were withdrawn early, with the last departing in 1956 but once more with high mileages. Marsh rebuilt four again with C3 boilers giving them a top heavy appearance and not a great improvement in performance. The higher centre of gravity also made them rough-riding. They nevertheless looked impressive and powerful.

The final class Billinton designed was a freight version of the E5 with 4'6" coupled wheels, so copying the E3s, but with vastly improved steaming so they could handle heavy goods traffic around London. Ironically like Stroudley, Billinton died before the first member of the class was completed and Douglas Earle Marsh completed the first example. Bradley describes the E6s as "first-rate goods engines and yard pilots" and they spent almost their entire lives in the roles for which they were designed. Once again C3 boilers were used to rebuild two and 32407/11 became E6Xs ("undoubtedly the best radial tanks of the LBSCR" Bradley states). They were long-lived, withdrawal commenced in 1957 and the final four departed in the "accountant's cull" in December 1962.

Stroudley's predecessor of the Radials was the 0-6-0T E1 class, some of which survived to BR days on shunting duties before E4s and then diesels replaced them. A number were allocated to Southampton Docks. Here No. 32606 is drifting along the street between West and East Docks with a transfer freight.. The driver is concentrating hard. It is probably 1950 - recently transferred from Brighton (the early British Railways on the side tanks confirms this early date) and the war damage in Southampton is still very obvious – Jones Furniture Stores and the Platform Tavern look somewhat woebegone! No. 32606 remained for the rest of her days at Southampton Docks (71I) until withdrawn in 1956.

THE FINAL YEARS OF THE BRIGHTON 'RADIALS'

Top - *No. 32479 at Brighton adjacent to the weigh house with behind the "New Shed" which finished as the Road Motor Engineer's workshop. 32479 looks pretty uncared for but would have been one of the allocation in regular use on the diagrams described in the article. Bradley describes its final days, "...in January 1963 No. 32474/9 were towed to Brighton from the Hove dump and restored to working order. 32479 shunted at Lewes and Newhaven." She proved to be the last survivor and after this brief reprieve was finally withdrawn in June 1963 and sent to Eastleigh for scrapping.*

Centre - *Two of the 70A contingent peep out bunker first from the shed accompanied by an M7. No. 32473 ex-Bricklayers Arms had arrived at Nine Elms in the summer of 1960, joining No. 32487, a previous regular at Guildford until re-allocation in 1958. In October 1962 Bradley records that No. 32473 was "worked down LE from Nine Elms to Horsted Keynes, with its BR lined black well-polished with the crests removed and carrying the number '473'." Now of course it is preserved and at times running as "Birch Grove" although more recently back in BR livery. Among its travels has been a trip to the Isle of Wight and the IOWSR, where it reproduced the failed attempt to employ an E4 on the island in 1947-49 when 32510 was resident at Newport.*

Bottom - *E6 No. 32408 at Feltham in 1961 – one of two transferred in November 1960 (with No. 32416). Employed on local shunting, the locomotives were scrapped in 1962. The photograph shows the tank engine buffer to buffer with No. 30495, a Urie LSWR G16 4-8-0T built for Feltham hump duties which were dieselised in 1954. Still employed into the 1960s with the H16s on transfer freights, by this time the big tank spent a lengthy period in store and was finally withdrawn in 1962.*

In the table that follow are some typical diagrams from BR days:

Locomotive Diagrams

Brighton MPD 75A

| 2PT/2FT (E4) | | 762 |

MO Stabled No 762 Sunday
MX Stabled previous day

---	Newhaven Loco	
5.55am //		
	Newhaven Middle Yard	
	F- Shunting	6.0 – 6.45
	F- Shunting	7.0 – 10.30
	C- Shunting	10.30 – 11.30
	F- Shunting	12.15pm – 1.20
	F- Shunting	2.0 – 6.0
---	Newhaven	
6.0pm //		
**	Newhaven Loco	

Stable for the next day

| 2PT/2FT (E4) | | 763 |

---	Brighton Loco	
6.32am //		
6.40am	Preston Park	
6.41am //		
6.45am	Hove	
7.1am F		
7.6am	Holland Road	
7.25am //		
---	Brighton Top Yard	
7.40am F		
9.15am	Falmer	---
	F- Shunting 9.25 – 10.10	
---	Falmer	
10.13am F		
11.15am	Brighton Top Yard	
11.32am F		
11.51	Kemp Town	

	F- Shunting 11.55 – 1.20	
---	Kemp Town	
1.29pm F		
1.54pm	Top Yard	

	F- Shunting 1.55 – 2.50	
---	Top Yard	
2.50pm //		
3.0pm	Brighton Loco	

	4.3pm //	
4.27pm	Lancing	5.31pm
P		
	assisting required A/R	
5.56pm	Brighton	
	6.22pm //	
6.34pm	Kingston Wharf	
	7.29pm F	

	(B)	
8.28pm	Preston Park	
	8.38pm F	
8.43pm	Brighton Top Yard	
	8.55pm	

	(Trip)	
**	Brighton Station	
	** //	
**	Brighton Loco	

Work No 766 next day

| 2PT/2FT (E4) | | 766 |

MO
---	Loco Yard	
2.55am //		
3.4am	Hove	

Pull out	P/O 3.50am F to Eastleigh	
---	Hove	
4.15am F		
and as MX		

MX
---	Loco Yard	
2.35am //		
2.40am	Top Yard	
3.0am F		
3.5am	Preston Park	
3.15am F		
3.21am	Hove	
4.15am F		
4.56am	Worthing Central	---
	F-Shunting 5.0- 8.15	
---	Worthing Central	
8.25am F		
	(6.32 ex Hove)	
9.0am	Angmering	

	F- Shunting 9.0 – 9.10	
	Angmering	
9.35am F		
9.46am	Littlehampton	---
	F- Shunting 9.50 – 10.10	

FX
---   Littlehampton
10.14am //
10.39am Chichester
11.13am V
1.27pm Brighton   ** //
**   Loco Yard

FO
                 F- Shunting 10.10 – 10.30
---   Littlehampton
11.40am //
12.31pm Brighton Loco   ---

Daily
---   Loco Yard
3.25pm //
---   Brighton   E
3.59pm P
5.0pm   Horsham
5.19pm P
6.21pm Brighton
6.49pm E
                 (off 1.0pm Cardiff)
6.55pm Hove
8.3pm //
8.26pm West Worthing   ---
                 F- Shunting 8.30 – 9.50
---   West Worthing
9.55pm F
10.5pm Worthing Central   ---

FX

                 F- Shunting 10.10 – 12.15
---   Worthing Central
1.15am F
1.45am Hove
1.50am //
2.0am   Brighton Loco

Work 763 next day

FO
                 F- Shunting 10.10 – 12.15am
And as shown 754 Sats.

2PT/2FT (E4)   Duty 767

---   Brighton Loco
6.17am //
6.23am Holland Road   6.58am

                 (propel)
7.2am   Brighton
7.10am P
7.33am Lancing   ---
                 C & WE shunting 7.45 – 5.0pm
---   Lancing
5.31pm P
5.56pm Brighton   6.0pm E
                 (propel)
6.6pm   Holland Road
6.38pm //
6.41pm Brighton Loco   ---

E6 No. 32417 after a lifetime at London sheds and a general overhaul at Ashford in 1959, eked out its final years at Brighton arriving as noted in the 'RO', "...in June 1961 from Bricklayers Arms." The photograph dates from either that summer or 1962 and the loco. was used on occasions on 75A duty 763, which included assisting with the "Lancing Belle". Here the author captured her shunting in Brighton shed yard, probably on the coal-stage pilot duty. No. 32418 was also on the books at this time. The crew are taking care as the engine is backed gently to haul the shed breakdown crane. The photograph captures the end of a life of 57 years that saw the E6 class change little, retaining their unique appearance to the end.

'IN FOR A SERVICE' / 'SOUTHERN INFRASTRUCTURE'

For it seemed decades the image of the steam engine was often that of the 'three-quarter' view, either at speed or on shed. Nothing wrong with that of course, but as a change we are delighted to present a few variations, based upon service and maintenance'

We continue with a few pages of infrastructure essential to keep the steam engine operating.

Bulleid's concept for the steam locomotive was to produce a machine that would be easy to prepare, and require minimal maintenance 'on shed'. An admirable philosophy indeed, let down partly by failing to ensure the infrastructure was in place to deal with the new design. Here we see two opposites, on the left and not withstanding the provision of TIA water treatment, boiler washouts were still required, albeit at far less frequent intervals. But who would envy the poor man atop the casing? Recorded at Nine Elms, the photographer has fortunately been present on a dry day, the thought of such work on a slippery casing in the face of lashing wind and rain is best not imagined.

Above is the opposite, and an idea that did work, no doubt also much appreciated by the men. This is the emptying of the ashpan, no more a task for the pit, a rake, hankerchief around the neck let alone grit in the eyes. Instead the simple alternative was to open the door whereupon all (well most) of the debris would fall conveniently into the pit.

'Southern Way' contributor Steve Godden contacted us earlier in the year to enquire whether we might be interested in viewing an album of images he had saved from the skip some years ago. (It is of course amazing what was recorded - but there are only so many gas valves and pieces of paperwork that can be shown.) BUT, included were a number of gems including these at Clapham Junction. No detail in the form of dates is given although it is mentioned that this particular type of water column was provided with an underground valve.

'IN FOR A SERVICE' / 'SOUTHERN INFRASTRUCTURE'

This time it is the turn of an unidentified 'Lord Nelson' to be the subject of the photographer. Two locations and two types of crane will be noted. Bottom on this page is certainly Nine Elms, but the second location is not so clear. What is interesting is that, with the shorter crane, it is necessary for the fireman to hold on to the hose to prevent it coming out of the tank. The idea of being soaked was hardly likely to appeal and certainly would incur the wrath of the driver operating the column on the ground.

Above - This is the first sight of Bournemouth West station that would greet a visitor. This shot was taken c.1962 some six years after a runaway train demolished the right hand corner of the parcels office. What is depicted here is the original Somerset and Dorset part of the station dating from 1874. Beneath the end of the awning is a suspended sign that is a reminds us of the railways' role which extended beyond the carriage of passenger and goods traffic: "Enquiries, Seat reservations and telegrams". The two parked cars in front of the luggage and parcels offices are of their time and are actually occupying the space designated for taxis but the delivery van parked outside the Queens Hotel has a decidedly vintage appeal.

Opposite - The full glory of the erstwhile Bournemouth West station is apparent in this picture. The building nearer the camera is the original one which served the S & D's two platforms in the station's early years, whilst the larger LSWR addition was joined to the original to form a comprehensive and elegant whole that served all six platforms after the extension to Bournemouth was opened in 1888. The entrance for passengers was beneath the ornate awning further from the camera.

REMEMBER BOURNEMOUTH?

Images by Michael Blackbourn*,
captions by Mike Morant,
text by M J Tarry

* unless indicated.

Above - *The track at the right hand edge of the picture serves platform 6 at Bournemouth West and the light patch beyond the buffer stop is in front of the damaged part of the parcels office caused by the runaway train on 17 August 1956. (See 'Southern Way Special Issue No. 8.') The cosmopolitan nature of Bournemouth's railways is evident here as the stock on the next track is headed by fleet No. M31035M which was an LMSR Diagram 2007 50' Brake Van built in 1939 at Wolverton whilst the vehicle to the left is an LNER Gresley era 61ft 6in Corridor Full Brake. The Morris Commercial J2 van, belongs to Sims the banana merchant, which company also occupied the goods shed at the time.*

REMEMBER BOURNEMOUTH?

My interest in railways started when I attended Boscombe Secondary School (Ashley Road, Boscombe, Bournemouth) from age 11 and cycled (three-speed Raleigh Sports – drop handle bars) to and from school via a lane which ran above Pokesdown station in a cutting. My family started off living in Seabourne Road at Fisherman's Walk over a cake shop, right opposite the trolleybus stop; then Father and Mother moved to Parkwood Road (they must have moved here before the war started as I can remember sleeping under the stairs during the blitz). Later this was run as a boarding house with summertime B & B & evening meal.

I and other friends used to stop opposite the signal box at Pokesdown to watch the trains pass by – two platform roads and two through roads. This was during WWII. We all hoped to see the big engines slip with their ten to twelve coach trains as they left westwards towards Boscombe. Post-war there was the Bournemouth Belle whilst other fast trains would speed through and down the bank towards Christchurch. In the opposite direction the climb would have freight trains labouring up Pokesdown bank, and, to us at least, just making it before the straight track through the station. Time was also spent talking (unofficially of course) to the signalman. Needless to say that all of us boys had our Ian Allan SR Loco Book where we would record the named locos seen - I never did find out what happened to my copy! With this interest there was little intention other than to be a railwayman and so, just prior to Christmas 1944, I attended the District Office (as arranged by the local station master) for interview and a medical. Everything went well and as a result I started as Junior Clerk at nearby Boscombe Station booking office (passenger, parcels and goods) in mid-January 1945, aged just 14 years, 3 months.

I was trained by two elderly gentlemen who taught me all about passenger, goods, and parcel office work and administration; plus of course the issue of tickets and waybills. They (the two elderly gentlemen – well, elderly to me at that time) were on alternate early and late turns with alternate Sundays. I worked a middle turn Monday to Friday plus a half-day on Saturdays. The station master was Mr T. Reed who was also in charge at Pokesdown and he was also one of life's true gentlemen. Of the two clerks, one, Mr Burroughs (I cannot remember the other one's name) used to have his hot lunch brought to him about midday, the turns changing over at 2.00 pm. I was usually given a tasty piece as well, notwithstanding the fact that I then went home for my own lunch. Both men smoked pipes, so together with the office fire the atmosphere inside the office can be imagined. As this was still wartime I can remember the soldiers' and tank trains passing through, several destined for, or departing from, Wool. There were also special workmen's trains, early and late, which were

always busy. Tickets for these services were available at a reduced rate for men going to Southampton Docks, Creekmoor Halt, or Holton Heath. Boscombe was not a busy station but it was the right place to learn, and all in all it was a happy time. Even though this was a suburb of Bournemouth we still had goods traffic: there was fruit traffic and also coal for Messrs. Belbens. I seem to recall there may also have been some container goods – Carter Paterson seems to be familiar. Boscombe was also the station used for supporters of the local football team, (the Cherries) whose home ground was at nearby Dean Court.

Having evidently established myself as competent it was not long before I was sent to relieve at Pokesdown on early (5.45am), middle (8.0am) and late (1.45pm) turns, each of these being of eight hours duration. Here we dealt with both passengers and parcels and it was quite busy. Pokesdown had a lady porter and me being young and a bit green I was caught with her going down in the lift whilst the others stopped the lift halfway. (No further comment will be made…) There were steep stairs to both the Up and Down platforms, so at times we had to take elderly passengers in the lifts. When on the middle turn I was quite often asked to go downstairs and help unload the fish train, en route from Grimsby, a smelly and unpleasant job for a 16-year-old clerk, the fish boxes being heavy and wet. Underneath the stairs to the down platform was the porters' room. I must have been doing things right as around 1946/47 I was promoted to Bournemouth West Station Master's Office (SMO) as pay clerk for all the staff including Branksome. Another part of the job was assisting the station master's clerk and sometimes relieving in the Enquiry Office as well as occasionally down at the town Information Bureau in Westover Road.

As pay clerk I had my own office upstairs next to the guards' room. There were over 100 staff whose wages I had to compile. In those days it was quite easy handling the various grades and their wages, including PAYE and other deductions. Even so, it paid to be careful, human nature was such that each man would check his wages carefully, hence complaints were normal but were usually quickly sorted out. I recall one day I was coming out of the SMO for an intended visit (the toilets were up the end of platform 4) and saw a ten-coach train coming down from the carriage sidings by gravity into No 5 road, I then saw the shunter jump clear as it appeared the handbrake was not working. The next thing was the front coach had hit and jumped over the stop-block, through the hoardings and out into the cab yard: fortunately there were no taxis present on that occasion. Since that day all empty trains were supposed to came down with the shunting engine attached.

The Bournemouth West .station master was Mr V.H. Jury, a gentleman of the old brigade, but a fair man at all times. Following the war Bournemouth West was

Opposite bottom - *An enlarged view of the brick built goods shed which stood in the yard on the east side of the station. By 1962 this had ceased to deal in conventional railway traffic and was leased to T. Sims (Banana Merchant) & Co. Ltd.*

The signal gantry controlling the exit from platforms 1 & 2 at Bournemouth West. In the background is Bournemouth West signal box that looked after movements through the narrow throat with which this station was afflicted. Just visible at the right edge of the picture is Maunsell 'U' class Mogul No. 31808 departing with an ECS working to the carriage sidings.

Ex-LSWR Drummond T9 'Greyhound' 4-4-0 No. 281 appears to be on station pilot duty at Bournemouth West in this post-war shot which could have been taken at any time before April 1949 when its BR identity of 30281 was applied. No. 281 was built at Nine Elms Works in 1899 and withdrawn in 1951 being finally allocated to Eastleigh. The depicted livery is unlined black with Bulleid's 'sunshine' characters; it is probable that No. 281 was a Dorchester-based engine when this shot was taken. Mike Morant collection

especially busy in the summer months with trains from the Midlands via the S & D, often full of workers having their annual holidays of a week or fortnight. It was interesting helping to work out the station programmes and getting them produced on the stencil printer, a messy job with purple ink. When time permitted, I sometimes tried my hand at train announcing. I enjoyed the work at Bournemouth West. It was a busy station open from 5.0am until midnight SX: Saturdays were different especially during the summer months.

Four signal boxes came under the supervision of the station: Station Box, West Junction, Gas Works Junction, plus Branksome – the last three being open continuously and known as the triangle. This triangle was useful, as by using it engines did not have to run light to the depot at Bournemouth Central. Branksome loco shed was also within easy reach for coal if required. The staff at the station included on the clerical side, the SM's clerk, booking office staff, enquiry office and of course me as pay clerk. Traffic (NUR) men included two inspectors, station foreman, signalmen, porter signalmen - who covered the gap

between early and late turns; shunters, porters, carriage-cleaning staff, parcels office staff, and I believe a dedicated goods porter plus a small goods office. We were mainly a passenger station with only one freight train daily, mainly coal which arrived via Branksome with the empties being returned; plus of course mail and parcels which came from Bath via the S & D. The afternoon mail left at 3.40pm and from a railway perspective was more important over the S & D than the down Pines Express. Nearby Branksome station had a booking clerk and platform staff. Around this time regular rest-days were introduced and as a result it was a problem covering the various grades, although this was overcome by 'step-ups' or overtime and then by specially designated 'relief' staff.

Despite its various carriage sidings, there was often a problem finding sufficient room to berth empty coaching stock during the peak holiday season and as a result recourse had to be made to outlying stations.

Railway service was interrupted by call-up and in November 1948 I went to the Royal Engineers - Group 145 at Cove, near Farnborough, ready for four weeks' square-bashing. After this I was posted to Longmoor to learn a trade - as a railway clerk! Following service overseas 'demob' came in May 1950 via Aldershot, but with it no job. The district office offered me a relief clerk's position pending a vacancy in the district office itself. Thus I travelled the district by cycle and relieved at various stations, usually for twelve-hour days. Amongst the locations I worked at were Wool, where I recall the SM was a vegetarian who offered me lunch (which of course I accepted), Broadstone, New Milton, Christchurch, and Millbrook Goods. At the last-named there was BAT and Toogoods' Seeds traffic, both generating plenty of waybills.

By 1951, I was in the district office Passenger Train Timetable Section checking train journals and sending out 'please explain' letters for extra time incurred at stations. Sometimes I would be an acting class 3 sending out notifications for short notice special trains. These would go out as a stencilled notice, rather than the being properly printed. Amongst the names recalled from this time were Mr Dear who was in charge, Mr Bright, and Mr Sparkes.

Several of the staff came from the west and we would travel on either the 7.37am or 7.47am from Pokesdown (the former if I got up in time, returning on the workers' train which left Souton (railway slang - Southampton) at 5.5pm. On this service there used to be quite a few of us and we used to play cards or have a nap and hope we didn't get carried past our stop.

Come 1955 there was the ASLEF strike which meant no trains and we could not get to work. Instead I reported to the nearest station which in my case now was Bournemouth Central where I was put in the SMO to assist. There were one or two trains manned by NUR staff but these only ran as and when men were available.

Later I was transferred to the Freight section and shortly afterwards together with a colleague we were given responsibility for the special freights running the next day during the week. These workings included the Fawley Oil / Petrol Block Trains from Esso, as advised by the SM, Fawley (Kit Carson) Furzebrook clay workings, and banana trains for Elders Fyffes. The banana train programme involved going up to London on the 7.20am ex-Bournemouth West from Southampton Central, then underground to the Elder Fyffes Office in company with the London West District man from the Woking Office. With luck, I came back to Southampton on the Belle, Waterloo at 12.30pm: failing that the 1.30pm train which didn't leave me much time to arrange the special notice in normal office times. There were 'Q' pathways in the freight timetable which were used for the banana specials, providing the special traffic section did not want these for boat train pathways off the various liners! There were also out-of-gauge loads - I was involved in the first movement of this type to Marchwood Power Station and the issue of a special notice to all concerned. Life was certainly never dull in those days.

Come the early 1960s and the Hampshire dieselisation scheme had commenced with regular interval trains which also made travel to and from work easier. Then the sky fell in and life was upset: Beeching occurred and everyone had their jobs altered.

Opposite page - *The photographer was standing on platform 2 at Bournemouth West when he took this interesting panorama. The two railway employees occupying a bench on platform 3 appear each to be reading a copy of the same document, which looks to be printed on foolscap paper folded four times. Adding to the interest in the foreground are three SR target station nameboards. The van in the background is fleet No. M31035M an LMSR Diagram 2007 50' Brake van built in 1939 at Wolverton.*

Above - Tucked away neatly in the northern corner of the goods yard at Bournemouth West was this neat brick-built water tower with, behind it and to the right, what seems to be a grounded coach body. However, it transpires, it is something quite different in the form of an LSWR Adams 30ft 6 wheeled passenger brake van of 1882-1885 complete with central caboose – the LSWR term for a birdcage.

Above - ECS workings from Bournemouth West station up to the carriage storage sidings was a feature of daily life as there was no engine release facility at the town end of the station for incoming locomotives. Awaiting departure from platform 4 with just such a movement is Maunsell 'U' class Mogul No. 31808, an Eastleigh allocated engine when this shot was taken. This is the stock from an incoming S&D train, the leading coach a Thompson era, but post-nationalisation built, Diagram 329 Corridor second from 1949 constructed by the Birmingham Carriage & Wagon.

Left - Bulleid 1st class restaurant car No. 7679 is the coach nearest the camera and which has a replacement door panel evident. This evening shot depicts another ECS working which will move the stock from an inbound Waterloo service away from Bournemouth West station and into the carriage sidings for servicing. This was a 1 in 90 starting climb for the motive power to cope with almost from the platform ends.

REMEMBER BOURNEMOUTH?

The Southampton and Woking District Offices were transferred to Wimbledon (except TSO). Staff either went to the new work abode, opted to become redundant, or moved to a local station to form a local skeleton staff ready to arrange day-by-day short notice specials. This was where I came under Mr Townroe. I did not want to go to London and instead opted for a complete change which resulted in my emigrating to New Zealand. But that really is another story!

Just setting out from platform 1 at Bournemouth West on the trek to Waterloo is Bulleid rebuilt West Country Pacific No. 34010 'Sidmouth', an engine which has proved to be something of a survivor albeit as a kit of parts spread around various sites in England. Fortunately there is every chance these parts will one day be reunited to form a complete working locomotive. No. 34010 was rebuilt in January 1959 and withdrawn in March 1965 whilst allocated to Nine Elms mpd as was the case when this shot was taken.

Opposite top - *Branksome hosted its own small servicing facility specifically for locomotives that had emanated from the Somerset & Dorset's metals but it also had an Achilles heel, insofar as whilst the turntable was long enough to accommodate the 2P 4-4-0's and 4F 0-6-0s, it was far too short for the S & D's 7F 2-8-0s and Stanier Black 5 4-6-0s. Those two classes were required to use the Branksome triangle as their turning method and here we see S & D 7F no. 53806 performing just such a manoeuvre in 1961.*
Mike Morant collection

Opposite bottom - *Pictures that feature Branksome mpd's environs are thin on the ground. This shot, taken from the window of a train bound for West station and with the shed and turntable out of shot to the right, depicts Fowler 2P 4-4-0 No. 40601 sporting the first incarnation of BR corporate branding which had been applied to this engine in October 1948. No. 40601 was not one of the batch from this class built specifically for the S&D but was nevertheless a resident of either Bath Green Park or Templecombe mpd from nationalisation until withdrawal whilst allocated to Bath in December 1959.*
Mike Morant collection

Above - *This picture illustrates the unusual positioning of the signal box high above the long down platform at the western end of Bournemouth Central, the advantage of which was a clear overview of the connection between the running lines and the shed environs. (Notice in particular the short forward walkway used by the signalman if he needed to communicate verbally with an engine crew or display a flag / lamp). Drummond M7 0-4-4T No. 40 had been transferred to Bournemouth mpd from Nine Elms in September 1941 and would remain there until April 1951. The livery shown here is plain black with Bulleid's 'sunshine' lettering which means that the shot was taken before its BR number 30040 was applied in March 1950. No. 30040 would spend time at Exmouth Junction and Plymouth Friary before returning to Bournemouth in May 1957 and remained there until withdrawn in June 1961.*
Mike Morant collection

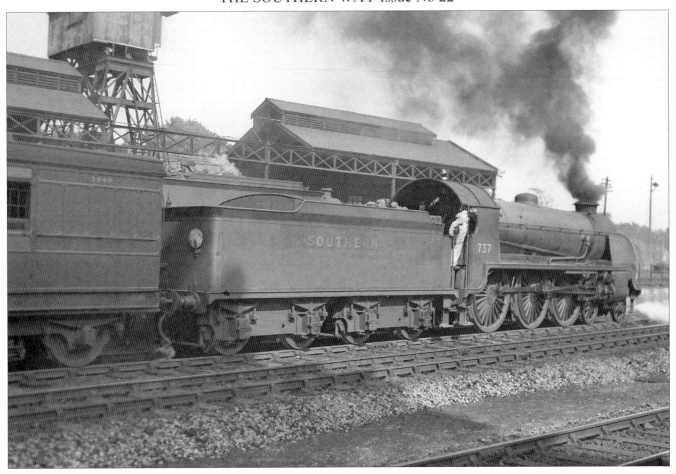

Above - Urie N15 class 4-6-0 No. 737 King Uther - Uther Pendragon was the father of King Arthur - passes the engine shed on the approach to Bournemouth Central station in 1947. No. 737 was of 1918 vintage and had been fitted with multiple blast pipes with wide chimney in 1941 whilst Bulleid's malachite livery with sunshine lettering was applied in October 1946, the engine at the time allocated to Eastleigh.. King Uther would be anointed with its BR number 30737 in June 1949, by now a Bournemouth engine and there 'she' would remain until withdrawal in June 1956.
Mike Morant collection

Opposite top - Bulleid original Merchant Navy Pacific No. 21C19 French Line C.G.T. had entered SR service in June 1945 and is depicted here in nearly sparkling condition at Bournemouth Central in 1947. The 'dolly' suggests that 21C19 is reversing in order to gain access to the shed whilst the begrimed rear of the tender side sheet tells us that this is a reversal from Bournemouth West following a journey down from Waterloo. 21C19 acquired its BR number, 35019, in March 1948 and would be a Nine Elms allocated engine for most of its relatively short working life. Transferred to Weymouth MPD in September 1964, withdrawal would be from that same shed a year thereafter.
Mike Morant collection

Opposite bottom - Views of Bournemouth shed and its environs photographed from the down platform are commonplace but panoramas such as this taken from the elevated signal box are much more scarce. The expected motive power for 1961 is depicted with Bulleid rebuilt WC Pacific 34040 Crewkerne, a couple of BR Standards and a Lord Nelson evident but arguably the most interesting hardware is the yard crane which was DS60 in the service stock list. It was built in 1923 using the chassis of redundant water tank LS10 which had seen earlier service behind an Adams engine. DS60 had a SWL capacity of 1.5 tons and was powered by electricity from a nearby fuse or switch box via an overground cable. Apparently, Dorchester and Horsham sheds had similar electrically powered cranes.

The spacious or even cavernous interior of Bournemouth Central station is evident in these two 1960s images with the general panorama still recognisable today even if the two centre tracks have been removed for over 40 years.

Opposite top - *Bulleid original West Country Pacific no. 34038 Lynton draws into Bournemouth Central with a northbound inter-regional working. No 34038 did not quite make it into the final year of Southern steam and was withdrawn from service at Nine Elms MPD in June 1966.*
Mike Morant collection

Opposite bottom - *A summer's day in 1961 and the photographer has taken the opportunity to capture the interior of Bournemouth Central station looking eastwards with a short goods train in the centre of the frame. The clock shows mid-morning, the early rush is over and now the station will quietly rest mainly until the arrival of the various down services from London The motive power, far from the camera, is an unidentified Maunsell S15 4-6-0.*

This page - *Someone has left the tap on! the last built Bulleid Q1 0-6-0 no. 33040, a Feltham allocated engine when this shot was taken, is depicted here on the up through road at the eastern end of Bournemouth Central with water streaming over the back of the tender.*

EVALUATING THE 'PEPs'

Simon Jeffs

During 1965, British Rail began planning their next generation of sliding-door electric multiple unit (EMU) trains to replace the ageing fleets of SUB, EPB and HAP stock that operated most of the inner suburban services on the South Western, South Eastern and Central divisions. Although suburban electric stock with air-operated sliding doors were universal on London Underground and had been introduced with the London Midland and Scottish Railway's

the commuter train
of the future

≷ Southern

"Wirral" (later Class 502) stock as early as 1938, the conservative Southern was still turning out 4-EPB units with compartments and slam doors as late as 1963. The new stock would be mechanically, electrically and aesthetically unlike anything that had operated on the Southern to date and its successful construction, introduction and acceptance by passengers would involve a vast amount of research.

Forty years on, it is hard to appreciate just what a quantum leap in internal design these units represented. Work was undertaken at the BR design centre in Derby at the same time as other iterations which included a double-deck unit carried on twin single-axle articulated bogies. So far as the Southern Region was concerned what emerged was a single-deck, sliding-door bodyshell with some similarities to London Transport's A60/62 surface stock. A wooden mock-up of a complete vehicle, including front end and cab, was erected at Doncaster and used for comparative loading and unloading tests with a slam-door vehicle. Authority was then given for the construction at BR Engineering York of two 4-car ("4-PEP") and one 2-car ("2-PEP") prototypes for extensive evaluation on the Southern Region, a 10-car rake being representative of maximum peak loadings on the South Eastern division's Dartford lines. Here, history repeated itself as the same routes were used to test Bulleid's 4-DD stock from 1949.

The features of the proposed units were presented to a conference at Derby on 19th/20th November 1970 by Messrs. Kibblewhite and Koffman in their paper "Future Policy for Suburban and Outer Suburban Trains" when it was made clear that they were seen as the blueprint for all future EMU suburban stock. The design was geared to short-distance commuting, with hard, low-backed, bus-style seating with thin, individual cushions, arranged 2+2 each side of a wide central gangway with many seat pairs arranged face to back. Such an arrangement provided greater standing capacity at the expense of seating. To add to the rapid transit ambience, the ceilings had hanging handholds, very similar to those found on London Underground tube stock. Lighting was by fluorescent tubes recessed in the ceiling and the internal paneling was of muted shades of grey or brown giving way to bright yellow in the doorway vestibules. Forced-air ventilation (**not** air-conditioning) was fitted in all three units. The first 4-car unit, 4001, had plain double-glazed windows, but this was rapidly found to be inadequate and these windows were replaced with conventional sliding glass panels, a feature perpetuated on the second 4-car unit, 4002 and the 2-car unit, 2001.

The first 4-PEP unit, 4001, was delivered to the Southern in May 1971, while the other units followed in

Left - The wooden mock-up at Derby.
Right - Loading/unloading trials (Photos: British Rail)

early 1972. Early work with the prototypes was mostly concerned with debugging the mechanicals and electrics but passengers finally got their chance to sample the new units when 4001 entered service on 4 June 1973 on the 11:43 Hampton Court-Waterloo. Due to restricted clearances, the units were restricted to services between Waterloo and Chessington South, Hampton Court and Shepperton. The complete 10-car rake also spent six weeks working selected services between Charing Cross/Cannon Street and Dartford *via* both the Sidcup and Bexleyheath routes and to Bromley North between August and September1973.

Almost immediately, the units attracted adverse comments. These particularly centered around (1) the lack of seats and their hard, uncomfortable nature and (2) the inadequate ventilation and heating. It was apparent that the engineering-led approach to the unit's design had not properly considered passengers' psychological and physiological reactions to the new travelling environment. The response of BR(SR) to this conundrum was to employ external consultants, Research Projects Limited (RPL), to carry out detailed research into these factors and make recommendations for changes to the production stock.

The basic approach taken by RPL was the relationship of the human body, seated and standing, to the environment

All three PEP units are seen at St Johns during the trials on the SE Division between August and September 1973 (SEG Foxley slide).

Top - *The first unit, 4001, shortly after arrival at Wimbledon Park (David Brown Collection)*

Middle - *The two-car unit at Waterloo (David Brown Collection)*

Bottom - *Two vehicles of No. 4001 at an Eastleigh Open Day in 1973 (Clinton Shaw)*

Opposite page - *No. 4002 at Waterloo East (David Brown Collection)*

presented by the PEP vehicles. RPL's remit from their clients (BR(SR)), was to "…establish customer reaction to the prototype train so that:-

a) Features that are most popular can be highlighted in local advertising campaigns.

b) Any desirable and feasible alterations can be incorporated into the production vehicles

c) Any features which are not well received but cannot be altered may be mitigated by appropriate publicity."

RPL carried out their initial fieldwork with the two 4-PEP units on the South Western Division between June and October 1973 on Waterloo-Shepperton / Hampton Court / Chessington South services, and, following the transfer of all three units to the South Eastern division, the full 10-car rake was assessed over a six-week period between August and September 1973 on Dartford line services. Following comments that seating conditions needed reassessment during the winter months, additional studies were undertaken between 7th -14th February 1974 on the South Western services listed above. All of the findings were compared to similar trials in contemporary suburban slam-door stock, SUBs, EPBs and HAPs (termed "EPB" stock in the reports). Three general research techniques were employed – Observational (by eye of 6000 passengers in summer and 2200 in winter plus filming of five selected

male and five female passengers in summer); Psychological – by in-depth interviews and questionnaires; Physiological (by heart-rate measurement of four male and three female passengers, plus temperature/humidity and noise readings). RPL's research was presented in two reports to BR(SR) in December 1973 and April 1974, covering their summer and winter fieldwork. Copies of these have recently been presented to the SEG archives and the rest of this article is concerned with their findings. Four key findings came from this research:-

1. The PEP stock was considered smoother and quieter than conventional EPB stock

2. The seat dimensions and design, and the contour of the PEP coaches produced MORE discomfort for both seating and standing passengers compared to EPB stock

3. The design objective of increased standing room was partially met but at the expense of sitting passengers and did not provide adequate comfort or support to standing passengers

4. Publicity should be educational, to explain the best ways of using the PEPs unique design features but should also set out the operational reasons for such features

The major part of the first report is devoted to a comprehensive

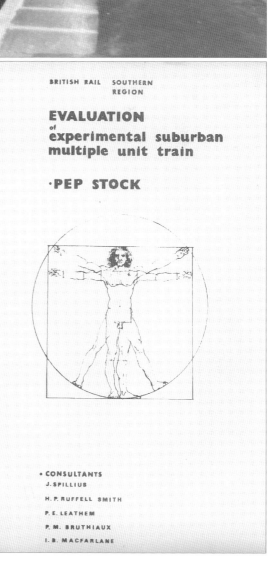

BRITISH RAIL SOUTHERN
REGION

EVALUATION
of
experimental suburban
multiple unit train

· PEP STOCK

· CONSULTANTS
J. SPILLIUS
H. P. RUFFELL SMITH
P. E. LEATHEM
P. M. BRUTHIAUX
I. B. MACFARLANE

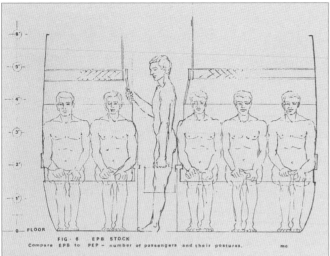

FIG. 6 EPB STOCK
Compare EPB to PEP – number of passengers and their postures. mc

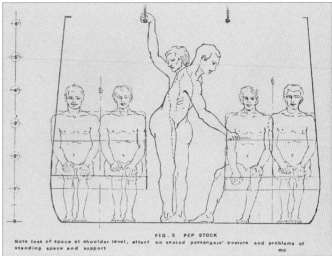

FIG. 5 PEP STOCK
Note loss of space at shoulder level, effect on seated passengers' posture and problems of standing space and support mc

analysis of passenger's responses to the design features. Regarding **noise**, all passengers felt that the ride of the PEP was smoother and quieter than EPB stock, predominantly due to the smooth riding of the DOC1 bogie and its associated active air suspension. Interior noise was further reduced by the use of sliding doors, with none of the "cerebral headache" effects caused by the incessant slamming of doors! The ease of conversation was "remarkable" compared to EPB stock. However, passengers' greatest ire was reserved for the **seating**, with a very small proportion favouring it over EPBs. The seats were felt to be uncomfortable, short at the back, not wide enough with no head rests or arm rests and the bus-seat design was considered claustrophobic and cramped. Passengers wanted a seat and would let a PEP train pass to obtain one in EPB stock. While there was more space for standing passengers, there was less for them to hold on to as the luggage racks were out of reach, the hanging straps were unstable and there were no vertical stanchions. This led standees to congregate in the door vestibules and not move down the aisles. A lot of the problems with the seating were due to its design. The seat cushions had an unacceptable angle of $85°$ between seat and back, rather than the $107°$ of EPB stock. This pushed passengers forward to adopt a "slumped" posture. When coupled with a reduced width of 36" compared to 39" and the inward-sloping profile of the bodysides, pushing passengers on the non-aisle seats inwards, it made for a very uncomfortable experience. In facing seats, the lack of space led to knees tangling in the middle encouraging passengers to twist and place their legs into the aisle, further reducing the space for standing passengers. Men adopted a far wider range of postures than women to minimize their discomfort. The situation was worse in winter, when passengers were wearing bulkier clothing. The diagrams below illustrate these postures, comparing "EPB Man" on the left to "PEP Man" on the right. Obviously, in peak hour conditions, it was more comfortable to travel naked!

The **heating and ventilation** systems also came in for severe criticism. Heat discomfort was severe during peak-hours and ventilation particularly poor for standing passengers. The small sample of heart-rate measurements indicated that this thermal stress was reflected in increased heart rate. However, a detailed analysis of the responses showed no real statistical differences in heat discomfort between PEP and EPB stock – it was too hot in both! Off-peak passengers tended to find the PEP stock "cooler", "airier" and "less stuffy". **Safety** was considered good in the PEPs, with the clear view down the carriage and train (once the inter-connecting doors were removed) being seen as positive. However, the power-assisted door closure and inability to open them in the event of an accident was negatively perceived. Still on **doors**, no difference was noted between the speed of detraining passengers between 2 - or 3-door variants per car; external handhold and handrails were required and the slightly crazy system of the door opening mechanism, whereby passengers were supposed to start the opening process themselves until the automation completed the process (leading to any passengers holding on to doors finding and that they were shutting!), was not liked!

A few other features were analysed. These units were the first to be fitted with **a public information system**. Passengers liked this, but train staff were reluctant to use it. The **luggage racks** were hopeless – too high (so could not use as handhold if standing) and too short. The **interior design** (except the seats) was liked. The open saloon gave an immediate impression of airiness, with a light, uncluttered interior. It was felt easier to keep clean, but 65% of respondents wanted ashtrays (how things have changed!) Various colours were tried on the bodysides and vestibules, with the brown hues used in 4001 favoured (very '70s!).

Finally, when the relevance of these design features to the commuter was examined, passengers did genuinely feel that BR was making "a brave attempt to improve their travel conditions" but the PEP design was not relevant to their needs because of the rotten seating and heating/ventilation. Off-peak passengers liked PEP stock as they could occupy

EVALUATING THE 'PEPs'

Right and below -
The clean, uncluttered interior of the PEP (unit 4001) – empty (above) and with passengers (right). But note the fixed windows, lack of handholds and small, high luggage racks. Even the trained BR Staff are sitting with discomfort. Note the men with knees into the aisle and twisted postures (British Rail)

two seats and experienced less strain regarding ventilation and heating, while reading/talking was far easier. However, the stark take-home message for BR was that PEP stock would only be favoured over EPB stock if seating and ventilation were improved and support for standees adequate. Comfort and functional design were more important than colours and appearance!

Before this design was to be considered for fleet production, a warning was given in the Kibblewhite and Koffman paper that the cost of such units was estimated to double and, as a result, "...considerable cheapening and reduction in performance may have to be accepted". This came to be most marked by the absence of air-conditioning, estimated to increase costs by about £3500 per vehicle (1970 prices) and to negate almost totally any weight savings provided by the use of aluminium bodyshells. So, as it was estimated that aircon would only be needed during 100 hours per year (compared to Rio de Janeiro!) it was not to be provided and suburban commuters have suffered ever since.

73

The Consultant's Recommendations

Following their research, RPL made three groups of recommendations, covering (I) PEP features they considered should be retained; (II) specific alterations that needed to be incorporated into fleet vehicles to reduce passengers' complaints and to better meet their needs; (III) linking features where there is interaction between them. It was accepted that there was no optimal solution to these problems and some recommendations could be cherry-picked according to the proposed usage of the fleet vehicles.

Fifteen recommendations were made in Group I. Keep the sliding doors, bogies and traction characteristics; allow free passage through the unit, keeping stanchions in vestibules, the wide windows, fluorescent lighting with diffusers, the public address system and the brown interior (yuk!): the glass-fibre seat shells were to be retained with detachable seat covers, angle of the seat shell (see Group II) and height above the floor plus the ribbed flooring in the vestibule.

However, the recommendations in Group II predicated some major changes, the first of which stated that the profile of the body shell should be altered to an approximation of EPB stock. As expected, the seating and provision for standing passengers needed radical modification. The profile of the seat cushion should conform to the profile of the seat shell and both the height and width of the seats should be increased. Vertical stanchions were required throughout the aisles and hand supports made available for passengers getting on and off trains. The gangway doors should be removed and the use of polyurethane discontinued. It was also accepted that passengers needed to be educated how to use the new trains! Interestingly, a lower priority recommendation was that a warning system should be devised to inform passengers when doors were opening or closing.

The interactive features covered in Group III were grouped into two clusters. First, the interactions between door type, door numbers, the choice between 2+2 or 3+2 seating and the aisle width will all impact on the speed with which passengers enter and exit the train. The second cluster was concerned with the interactions between heating, ventilation, the presence or absence of aircon, sealed windows or sliding lights and the use of fail-safe systems to provide air in the event of power failure. Such metanalyses were not the domain of engineers in those days and this is a good, early example of a consideration of the "total train environment".

Modifications to the Prototypes

Obviously, not all of these features could be tested in the prototypes, but sliding lights were rapidly provided in the windows of 4001 in service and 4002/2001 before entering passenger service. However, the windows next to the cabs could not be altered due to the sliding door pocket of the drivers cab. Compare No. 4001 at Wimbledon Park in 1973 (top: *photo **James Dixon***) with the same unit in departmental service (renumbered as No. 056) in late 1976 (*bottom: photo **SEG Collection***). In addition, white external handles were fitted to the doors, clearly visible on No. 056.

Loading trials had shown that a third door was not needed in each vehicle and this was sealed out of use prior to the trials on South Eastern, but enhanced publicity regarding door operation was rolled-out there and reduced the learning period with doors from 2-3 weeks on South Western to 3-4 days on South Eastern. The best way to do this was leaving leaflets on seats – after four days, saturation coverage had been achieved! Oh, and RPL recommended not calling them prototypes, as this implied nothing could be modified. "Experimental trains" was better.

What Happened to the PEPs?

Late in 1973, one driving car from 2001 was swapped for that of No. 4001 giving both an unpainted car (right) (*photo: Donald McDonald*)) and, shortly after, 2001 was taken out of passenger service, leaving the SR for Derby in 1974. Here, it was fitted with an intermediate trailer car with a 25kV pantograph, and used as the test bed for both the dual-voltage Class 313 and 25kV overhead Class 314 units, spending time in both East Anglia and Glasgow. It was eventually scrapped in 1987. 4001/2 were transferred to Departmental stock at the end of 1976 and renumbered (935) Nos. 056 and 057 respectively. No. 057 was quite extensively used in new bogie tests and even received a prototype APT livery in 1980 (*below, photo David Brown Collection*). No. 057 was eventually stored in Clapham Junction yard from March 1983 and scrapped in

1989. No. 056 was unsuccessfully tried out as a depot shunter at East Wimbledon but was moved to Derby before being broken up in 1986.

Fleet Production

The first production units developed from the PEPs were the dual-voltage Class 313 units that went into service on the Great Northern electrification scheme in 1976 and the Class 314 25kV overhead units that were delivered to Glasgow from 1979. The production units for the Southern Region were Class 508, produced after an almost identical batch of Class 507 units for Merseyside. A final batch,

Class	Introduction/ Numbering	Initial Area	Current Status (2012)	Franchises (number) (2012)
313	1976 -64 units	Great Northern	All in service. 16 to Euston-Watford 1997-2001; 19 to Southern 2010	First Capital Connect (44) Southern (19) Network Rail (1)
314	1979 – 16 units	Glasgow suburban	All in service	Scotrail (16)
315	1980 – 61 units	Great Eastern suburban	All in service	Abelio (Greater Anglia) (61)
507	1978 – 33 units	Merseyside	32 in service. 1 unit withdrawn	Merseyrail (32)
508	1979 – 43 units	Southern (South West Division)	Transferred to Merseyrail by 1984. 12 x 508/2 to Southeastern 1996 – now stored OOU. 3 x 508/3 to Silverlink 2003 – now stored OOU. 1 unit withdrawn	Merseyrail (27) Stored (15)

Class 315, went into service on the former Great Eastern Liverpool Street - Shenfield lines Details of these fleets are tabulated above.

And were the lessons of the consultants learned? By and large, yes. The bodyshell was modified to give a more comfortable profile and to consign "PEP Man" to history, only two sliding doors per vehicle were fitted, double-glazed windows came with an opening section, pressure ventilation was installed (no expensive aircon) and plenty of stanchions and grips were provided for standing passengers. Liked by some, loathed by others, the low-backed, hard seats in their shells were used throughout the fleets in 2+3 facing mode except around the doors where they reverted to 2+2. The ride was comfortable on the new bogies with air suspension and the interior design modern and bright. First into service were the 313 units. These dual voltage (750v dc third rail/25kV ac overhead) were introduced in a blaze of publicity onto the newly-electrified Great Northern suburban services between Kings Cross/ Moorgate-Welwyn Garden City/Hertford with the claim that the "...new trains will be amongst the best of their kind in the world" and had been developed "...following a research

programme which was the most extensive ever carried-out on inner-suburban train design in Britain". While the second statement had a ring of truth about it, the first is open to debate! One major change from the PEPs was that power bogies were located under the driving cars, four GEC G310AZ traction motors being provided on each end vehicle. Rated at 111hp each, the units were certainly nippy, reaching 60mph from a standing start in 1½ minutes. Hopper windows were provided, but later were partially blocked to stop the local yobs throwing the seat cushions on to the lineside. One bad feature perpetuated from the PEPs was the use of the passenger door opening mechanism. This was rapidly knackered, the handles plated over and door opening reverted to Guard control. Next into service were the Class 314 units for the Glasgow suburban lines Rutherglen electrification that joined the systems north and south of the Clyde. Until recent (2011) refurbishment, the interior of these units were untouched. Note the stanchions, hopper windows, low-backed 3 + 2 seating, fluorescent lighting and hand rail on the front edge of the luggage rack (*left: Photo 'GB'*). However, the lessons concerning the door-opening mechanisms had been learned and these, and all subsequent fleet units, reverted to Guard control. In recent years, door-opening has reverted to passenger control, with DDR-compliant buttons and signage in most units. The remaining fleets followed the pattern of the 314s and have proved exceptionally reliable. Following their displacement from Watford-Euston duties by Class 378 units, 16 Class 313 units (plus 3 from FCC) were transferred to Southern to operate Coastway services centered on Brighton. The refurbishment was of very high quality, with high-backed seats arranged 2+2 and, although there have been some complaints about the lack of toilets, the units are admirably suited for short-distance duties.

At the current time, most of the fleet remains in service or stored. Only two units have been withdrawn, although replacements for the Merseyrail fleet will be in service before 2018. The latest (2011) "Golden Spanner" awards for reliability gave the Class 315 fleet a Silver

Following their displacement from Watford-Euston duties by Class 378 units, 16 Class 313 units (plus 3 from FCC) were transferred to Southern to operate Coastway services centered on Brighton. The refurbishment was of very high quality, with high-backed seats arranged 2+2 and, although there have been some complaints about the lack of toilets, the units are admirably suited for short-distance duties. Left - Door in Class 315 unit: Photo Colin Duff, Right 'GB'.

Spanner award for most-improved fleet amongst the ex-BR EMUs. The FCC 313s did well too, although the Class 507/8s are now showing their age and the Scottish 314s came bottom of the league. However, the latter are now undergoing extensive refurbishment.

There is no doubt that the extensive research that went into both the engineering and passenger environment of the PEPs set new standards for suburban train design. The PEP interior design has lasted well and, although high-backed seats are now in favour, it has adapted easily to modern commuting requirements. On the Southern, it initiated the replacement of the slam-door 'EPB' fleets and, although the 508s were not well-received, the subsequent Class 455 design which adopted and

evolved many of the PEP features, is now the most reliable ex-BR EMU in service and, like the PEP fleets, has been dynamically refurbished to provide an interior that will suit it for commuter usage for many years to come.

Right *- Still going. 313 219 at Seaford on 5 June 2012 (Photo: Simon Shreeve)*

Remember the 'COR's?

Displaced by more modern electric trains on the Portsmouth line, the remaining 4COR sets found their last use relegated to local services. Here and on page 80, set No 3153 is recorded at Frimley whilst forming a Guildford to Waterloo service on 23 October 1971.

Photographs by Paul Cooper

SOUTHERN EPHEMERA

WE ARE DELIGHTED TO PRESENT A FURTHER SELECTION FROM THE FASCINATING COLLECTION OF SOUTHERN AND CONSTITUENT PAPERWORK COURTESY OF MICHAEL BROOKS.

(An initial selection appeared in SW21.)

Above - Publicity for the introduction of the 4BUF units which complemented the 4COR sets from 1937/8 in connection with the electrification of the Mid-Sussex line. The artist is remarkably accurate; reference the interior with the correct ten stools shown and two of the four groups of four unclassified 'buffet seats'. There was always a trade-off reference making the interior attractive and inviting but not encouraging the punter to dawdle for too long. At the right hand end of the vehicle were two lavatories.

HAVE A DAY OFF!

ON THE ELECTRIC COAST . . .

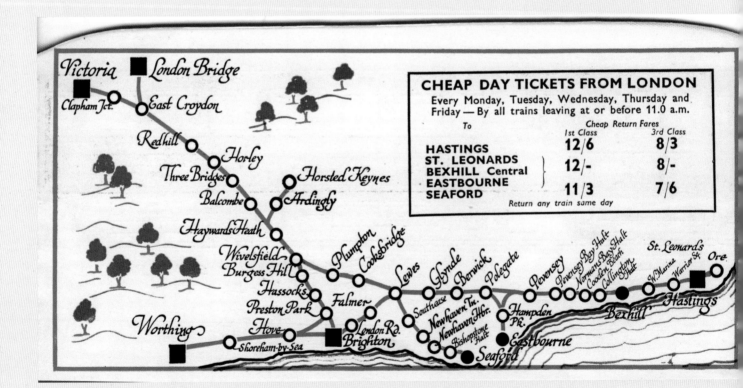

CHEAP DAY TICKETS FROM LONDON

Every Monday, Tuesday, Wednesday, Thursday and Friday — By all trains leaving at or before 11.0 a.m.

To	Cheap Return Fares	
	1st Class	3rd Class
HASTINGS	12/6	8/3
ST. LEONARDS		
BEXHILL Central }	12/-	8/-
EASTBOURNE		
SEAFORD	11/3	7/6

Return any train same day

Undated (but possibly 1935) fold-out brochure for cheap-day tickets. This time the artist has been less than kind with the 'coach' somewhat out of proportion. When completely open the formation resembled a 6-car CIT/PUL set, although its crudity makes exact identification impossible.

Circular Tours
BY RAIL
from LONDON

THROUGH
SOUTHERN
ENGLAND

Famous Cities
Finest Scenery
Fashionable
Resorts.

"Easy Tour" Travel
by
SOUTHERN RAILWAY

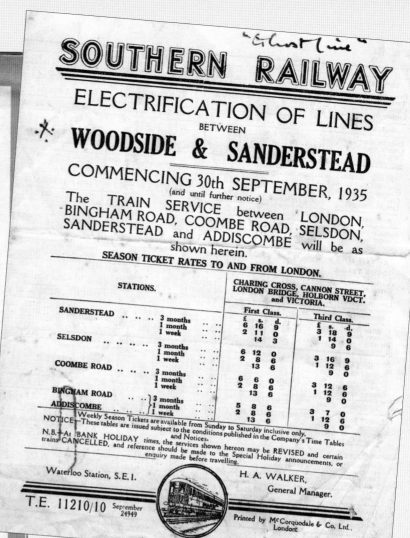

SOUTHERN RAILWAY
ELECTRIFICATION OF LINES
BETWEEN
WOODSIDE & SANDERSTEAD
COMMENCING 30th SEPTEMBER, 1935
(and until further notice)

The TRAIN SERVICE between LONDON, BINGHAM ROAD, COOMBE ROAD, SELSDON, SANDERSTEAD and ADDISCOMBE will be as shown herein.

SEASON TICKET RATES TO AND FROM LONDON.

STATIONS.		CHARING CROSS, CANNON STREET, LONDON BRIDGE, HOLBORN VDCT. and VICTORIA.					
		First Class.			Third Class.		
		£	s.	d.	£	s.	d.
SANDERSTEAD	3 months	6	16	9	3	18	0
	1 month	2	11	0	1	14	9
	1 week		14	3		9	6
SELSDON	3 months	6	12	0	3	16	9
	1 month	2	8	6	1	12	9
	1 week		13	6		9	0
COOMBE ROAD	3 months	6	6	0	3	12	6
	1 month	2	8	6	1	12	6
	1 week		13	6		9	0
BINGHAM ROAD	3 months	5	8	6	3	7	0
ADDISCOMBE	1 month	2	8	6	1	12	6
	1 week		13	6		9	0

NOTICE—Weekly Season Tickets are available from Sunday to Saturday inclusive only, These tables are issued subject to the conditions published in the Company's Time Tables and Notices.

N.B.—At BANK HOLIDAY times, the services shown hereon may be REVISED and certain trains CANCELLED, and reference should be made to the Special Holiday announcements, or enquiry made before travelling.

Waterloo Station, S.E.1.

H. A. WALKER,
General Manager.

T.E. 11210/10 September 24949

Printed by McCorquodale & Co. Ltd. London.

The handbill above is self explanatory although the front cover of the brochure on the left is altogether more interesting. It is in fact no less than a list of 24 'tours' possible by rail and which may well be taken to be similar to the BR 'Railway Roundabout' tickets of later years, albeit it appears for a single day only.

Targetting the visitor from abroad, the routes that might be taken were certainly interesting, one example being 'Tour No 10 - Sussex and Hants'. From London the route was, Hastings-Bexhill-Eastbourne-Brighton-Chichester-Southampton-Bournemouth-London' The fare was 50/- 1st and 30/- third.

Potential passengers were enticed or lured by places of interest of en route - breaks of journey were permitted - but in reality how much time would the trip itself have taken as these 'tours' were made by ordinary scheduled services?

Equally difficult was when a tour involved travel on a line where the service might well have been somewhat sporadic, this included the S & D and between Salisbury and Wimborne. There was also an Isle of Wight tour that required travel between Ventnor and Newport and then Newport to Yarmouth.

But this was nothing compared with Tour No 17, 'Hants, Wilts, Somerset, Gloucester and the Shakespeare Country'. The itinerary was: London-Winchester-Salisbury-Glastonbury-Wells-Bath-Bristol-Gloucester-Worcester-Stratford on Avon-Warwick-Kenilworth-Oxford-London'. All for 65/6 or 39/6 and in one day - surely not.

Going back in time the collection revealed an example of the first timetable for the 'Elevated Electric Railway' together with that of the late southwards extension (- wish we had known of these when we did the pictorial work in 2011!)

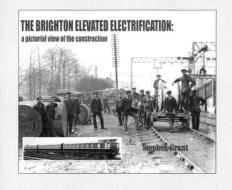

THE SOUTH LONDON ELEVATED ELECTRIC RAILWAY.

The line now electrified is known as the South London Line, and extends from Victoria to London Bridge, via Battersea Park, Wandsworth Road, Clapham, East Brixton, Denmark Hill, Peckham Rye, Queen's Road, Old Kent Road, and South Bermondsey, and is just under nine miles in length.

Inside Victoria Station seven lines are equipped with overhead construction, giving access to five platforms, and in London Bridge Station, five platforms are similarly fitted.

The time taken by the steam trains from Victoria to London Bridge is 36 minutes; the electric trains reduce this to 24 minutes.

The system adopted is known as the single-phase alternating high tension system of electrification, and involves the use of overhead conductors, which are supported from two steel cables, and the Brighton Railway is the first to adopt it in England.

The current is collected by means of what is known as a collector bow, fixed to the top of the cars, being pressed against the overhead copper contact wire.

Contrary to all the other electric railway companies, who have adopted the American type of coaches, with end doors, the Brighton Railway has adopted side door corridor carriages, which, it is believed, will prove more satisfactory to the travelling public and all concerned, as the design embodies all the advantages of the compartment carriage without its disadvantages. The third class coaches have eight passenger compartments, and seat 72 passengers. The first class coach comprises nine compartments, and seats 74 passengers. The seating capacity per train is therefore 218 passengers. No second class accommodation will be provided.

In order to provide for even distribution of passengers, each carriage has a gangway arranged half way down each side.

Ample parcel and umbrella racks are provided, and all the trains are handsomely upholstered, and at night are brilliantly lighted.

Every thing that human forethought can do, has been done, to provide for the comfort and safety of the passengers, and the public will find the newly electrified South London Line a cheap, speedy, and comfortable means of reaching the City and West End.

Waterlow & Sons Limited, Printers, London Wall, London.

West Sussex Railway
(Selsey Tramways Section).

NOTICE.

UNTIL FURTHER NOTICE

A Late Train

WILL RUN

EVERY WEDNESDAY

FROM

Selsey to Chichester

AND BACK,

AT THE FOLLOWING TIMES, VIZ:

Depart SELSEY...	...	7.15 p.m.
Arrive CHICHESTER	...	7.45 p.m.
Depart CHICHESTER	...	10.30 p.m.
Arrive SELSEY ...	...	11.0 p.m.

Return Fare 1/-.

Accommodation is limited— Please therefore book early.

AN OPPORTUNITY TO VISIT THE CINEMA AND SUPPORT THE LOCAL LINE.

BY ORDER.

Selsey, November, 1931.

S. C. Jennings & Sons, Ltd., Redhill.

Kent & East Sussex, Shropshire and Montgomeryshire, Rye & Camber, Selsey (West Sussex) Weston, Clevedon & Portishead, and East Kent Lines.

GENERAL PASS, 1922.

GENERAL FREE PASS.

1922.

FIRST CLASS.

No. **31**   FREE PASS.
FIRST CLASS.
Available to 31st December, 1922.
(Unless previously cancelled or withdrawn.)
AVAILABLE BETWEEN
ANY STATIONS
On Kent and East Sussex, Shropshire & Montgomeryshire, Rye and Camber, Selsey (West Sussex), Weston, Clevedon and Portishead, and East Kent Lines.

Issued to *Lt. Col. David Davies*

The use of this Pass is restricted to the person to whom it is granted, and it will be forfeited if transferred. Any other person using it will be liable to the Penalties incurred by a Passenger travelling without having paid his fare. The Pass is to be exhibited and given up when required, and is issued free, and so accepted by the holder on condition that he undertakes all risks, loss or injury to himself or his luggage, however caused, and that he is subject to the Company's Bye-laws and Regulations.

SUPPORT THE LOCAL LINE.

WEST SUSSEX RAILWAY.

(Selsey Tramway Section).

Easter Holidays.

1932

ON
THURSDAY, March 24th & SATURDAY, March 26th,
The following Service of Trains will run :—

DOWN.	a.m.	a.m.	p.m.	p.m.	p.m.	p.m.	p.m.
Chichester ...dep.	9 15	1130	2 10	4 10	5 50	7 15	8 40
Selsey Town arr.	9 45	1212	2 40	4 40	6 20	7 45	9 10

UP.	a.m.	a.m.	p.m.	p.m.	p.m.	p.m.	p.m.
Selsey Town dep.	8 10	10 0	1 10	3 10	5 10	6 25	8 0
Chichester ...arr.	8 40	1040	1 40	3 40	5 40	6 55	8 30

On GOOD FRIDAY and EASTER SUNDAY,

The following Special Service of Trains will run :—

DOWN.	a.m.	a.m.	p.m.	p.m.	p.m.
Chichester ...dep.	9 30	1130	2 20	6 10	8 10
Selsey Town arr.	10 0	12 0	2 50	6 40	8 40

UP.	a.m.	a.m.	p.m.	p.m.	p.m.
Selsey Town dep.	8 50	1010	1 40	5 10	7 5
Chichester ...arr.	9 20	1040	2 10	5 40	7 35

On EASTER MONDAY, March 28th,

The following Special Service of Trains will run :—

DOWN.	a.m.	a.m.	a.m.	p.m.	p.m.	p.m.	p.m.	p.m.
Chichester ...dep.	915	1050	1210	2 20	5 10	6 35	8 25	10 0
Selsey Town arr.	945	1120	1240	2 50	5 40	7 5	8 55	1030

UP.	a.m.	a.m.	a.m.	p.m.	p.m.	p.m.	p.m.	p.m.
Selsey Town dep.	830	10 0	1130	1 25	4 30	5 50	7 20	9 5
Chichester ...arr.	9 0	1030	12 0	1 55	5 0	6 20	7 50	9 35

On TUESDAY, March 29th,

The Ordinary Service of Trains will run.

CHEAP DAY TICKETS will be issued on all Trains between **CHICHESTER** and **SELSEY**, available for return on day of issue only.   **RETURN FARE 1/-** (Children under 14 years of age Half Fare).

CHEAP DAY RETURN TICKETS will be issued from SELSEY TOWN to ARUNDEL (2s. 5d.), BOGNOR REGIS (2s. 2d.), BRIGHTON (4s. 5d.), FRATTON (2s. 11d.), HOVE (4s. 5d.), PORTSMOUTH and SOUTHSEA (2s. 11d.), and WORTHING (3s. 2d.), by all Trains allowing of Return same day.

Selsey Town, March, 1932.   *BY ORDER.*

WEST SUSSEX RAILWAY

3

From ....

To ....

Via ....

No. of Truck .... Owner ....

Date .... 193......

Consignee ....

Paperwork from some of the lesser railways is especially pleasing, from a personal perspective the West Sussex Railway, aka 'The Selsey Tram' particularly so.

Notwithstanding the examples of the general everyday paperwork seen, it cannot be denied the line was not attempting to attract extra passengers, as per the Wednesday late train. On the same notice it is interesting to note the requirement to 'book early' - whether anyone did is another matter! It was a brave attempt, likewise the Easter Holiday timetable for the following year.

The 'General' free pass for the various destinations encompasses the complete Col Holman Stephens empire, but who was Lt Col David Davies?

HUNDRED OF MANHOOD AND SELSEY TRAMWAYS COMPANY, LTD.
REVISED PARCELS RATES.
The rates for conveyance of Parcels by Passenger Train between any pair of Stations on the Selsey Tramways, including delivery at Selsey within the ordinary limits, are as follows :—

WEIGHT NOT EXCEEDING

7lbs.	14lbs.	28lbs.	42lbs.	56lbs.	84lbs.	112lbs.
4d.	5d.	6d.	8d.	10d.	1s. 0d.	1s. 2d. each.

and an additional 2d. for every 14lbs. or portion of 14lbs. above 112lbs.

SMALL CONSIGNMENTS OF GOODS.
The Station to Station charges for conveyance of small consignments by Goods Train on the Selsey Tramways are as follows :—

RATE NOT EXCEEDING.	WEIGHT NOT EXCEEDING.								WEIGHT ABOVE 5 CWT.
	1 qr.	2 qr.	3 qr.	1 cwt.	1½ cwts.	2 cwts.	2½ cwts.	3 to 5 cwts.	
	s. d.	s. d.	s. d.	s. d.	s. d.	s. d.	s. d.	s. d.	
7/6 per ton	0 3	0 5	0 7	0 9	1 0	1 3	1 6	1 9	Actual Calculation
8/4 per ton	0 3	0 5	0 7	0 9	1 0	1 4	1 9	2 1	Actual Calculation
11/8 per ton	0 4	0 6	0 8	1 1	1 4	1 10	2 4	2 6	Actual Calculation

Full list of Goods Rates will be forwarded upon application.

Special rates will be quoted for guaranteed tonnage. For particulars apply to Superintendent's Office, Selsey. G. ECKFORD, Superintendent.

West Sussex Railway (Selsey Tramway Section.)

.................................—Station, Sussex.

Mr..   ....193...

The undermentioned goods have arrived at this Station in your name. If not removed by 5 p.m. on ...., demurrage at the rate of................per truck and 6d. per sheet for each of the first two days (or part of a day), and 5/- per truck and 1/- per sheet for each subsequent day (or part of a day), or siding rent at the rate of 6d. per truck per day will be charged for detention.

The goods remain on hand at owner's risk and expense.   **A. W. SMITH.**

Truck No.	From	Description.	T.	C.	Q. Lbs.	TO PAY. £ s. d.

ONE OF
THE MANY
BEAUTY SPOTS

CLOVELLY
from Hobby
Drive...

REACHED
BY THE
L & S.W.R

CHAS. J. OWENS, General Manager.

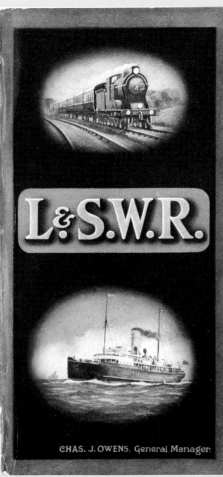

L.&.S.W.R.

CHAS. J. OWENS, General Manager.

HOLIDAY TRIPS
VIA SOUTHAMPTON

BY DAY & NIGHT
ACROSS THE CHANNEL

CHAS. J. OWENS, General Manager.

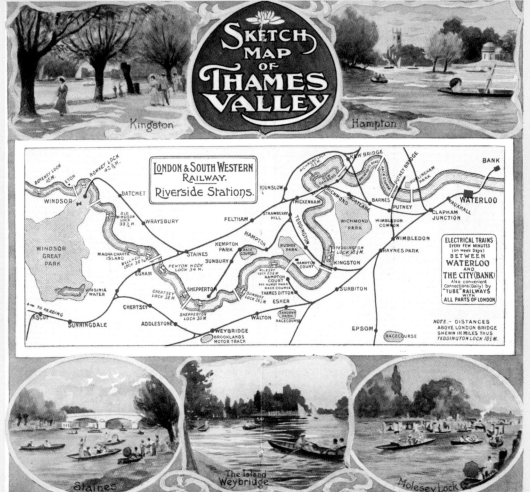

SKETCH
MAP
OF
THAMES
VALLEY

Kingston

Hampton

LONDON & SOUTH WESTERN
RAILWAY.
Riverside Stations.

ELECTRICAL TRAINS
Every Few Minutes
(on week Days)
BETWEEN
WATERLOO
AND
THE CITY (BANK)
Also convenient
Connections (Daily) by
"TUBE" RAILWAYS
WITH
ALL PARTS OF LONDON

NOTE.— DISTANCES
ABOVE LONDON BRIDGE
SHEWN IN MILES THUS
TEDDINGTON LOCK 18½ M.

Staines

The Island
Weybridge

Molesey Lock

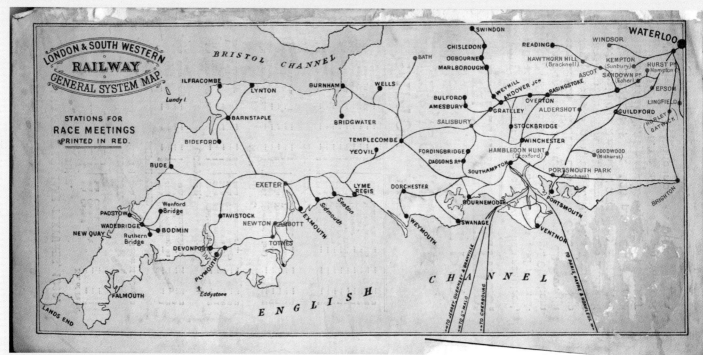

Now it is the turn of the LSWR to get in on the act with some wonderful examples of holiday and excursion brochures.

The interior of the Holiday Trips across the Channel showed connections to the port from throughout the UK - conveniently ignoring of course the shorter passage via Dover / Folkestone.

Equally interesting is the map indicating the locations of the various race meetings - notice also the Hambledon Hunt at Droxford on the Meon Valley line. Within were various timetables showing how most (but certainly not all) of the locations might be reached including connecting services off some of the more obscure branches.

In reply to your

Refer hereto in your reply

LEE-ON-THE-SOLENT RAILWAY.

LEE-ON-THE-SOLENT STATION. *To* *Date*

Address: Station Master.

Subject ______________________________

Finally, a letterheading from another obscure railway and then…….'anyone fancy dinner with Mr Stroudley…?'

Fairlight,
Preston Road,
Brighton, 31st March, 1877.

Sir,

Will you do me the honour to dine with me, my Foremen, and a few friends, at the Old Ship Hotel, Brighton, at 6.30 for 7 p.m., on Friday the 13th of April, on the occasion of the completion of the 100th New Locomotive since my appointment to the Brighton Railway in 1870?

An early answer will oblige,

Yours faithfully,

W. Stroudley.

D. Jones Esqr
Inverness

MOMENTS

Left - Barry Coom (see Woking Homes article in SW8) arrived recently with a small album containing six portraits of the former Orphanage collecting dog from Exeter. Other than the photographer's name, 'Chandler', no name for the dog was given - one wonders if this was the animal that used to walk through the train at Exeter Queen Street collecting as he went? Whatever, a fine specimen.

Below - The Basingstoke snow plough, known to have been of LSWR vintage but seemingly rarely photographed other than in one official LSWR broadside view with the background deliberately painted out. Here the same fascinating vehicle is clearly recorded in SR times, but how long did it last, were there others, and was it, as appears, almost a wooden body placed upon a 4-wheel underframe? In which case were there additional weights in or under the chassis? The dumb buffer beam will be noted. (Answers on a post card please......) We look forward to learned comment.

Terry Cole's Rolling Stock File No. 22

SECR 'Birdcage' Brakes

The SECR and its constituents were not alone amongst the pregrouping companies in being wedded to having a 'Birdcage' lookout for the guard atop his compartment, but they were probably its most prolific and sustained user.

This was no doubt in part due to the width restrictions on many of its lines which made the use of the side ducket favoured by many other railways, difficult. Early brake coaches were quite short, but lengths gradually increased over time with the final examples being nearly 64ft long overall. That is much longer than a Maunsell coach and not a lot shorter than a Bulleid or BR Mark 1! It was only after Wainwright had resigned that the 'Birdcage' was finally abandoned and the last three-coach sets entered traffic from 1915 without them. A fully restored birdcage coach is now running on the Bluebell Railway so one of these typical SECR vehicles can now be seen once more.

This is a three-compartment Third Brake seen here in Departmental use at Wadebridge on 24 August 1960. This type of Birdcage coach is easily recognised by its short length and slatted louvres on the van windows with toplights above. Its overall body length was 45ft (48ft 11½ in over buffers). This vehicle seems to have an extra window between the compartments and the van doors which is probably a lavatory with which Nos. 2297/8 were originally fitted. They also had a side corridor allowing the compartments access to this lavatory. This vehicle could therefore be No. 2298 which became SR No. 3245 (Diagram 143) and which was transferred to the Loco Dept at Dover in 1944 as No. 1969s. A total of 22 vehicles were built by the Met. RC&W Co. in 1900/1, although the SECR, apparently not content with having so many similar vehicles, rebuilt two almost immediately as 1st class saloon brakes, one as a 2nd class brake and one as a composite brake! Two also had a lavatory and a side corridor. No. 1969s was withdrawn in 1964.

Right - Here is another short Birdcage brake, this time with six compartments and overall length 53ft 10in. As SECR No. 1061 this was one of 14 composite brakes with five third-class compartments and one second built as part of a batch of three-coach sets in 1909. These were to replace antiquated stock on the London outer suburban services. Originally in SECR set No. 102 it was renumbered No. 3334 by the Southern in set No. 541. In 1952 it was transferred to the service stock as DS 3208 and is seen here at Surbiton on 4 March 1960. After withdrawal it was purchased by the Bluebell Railway where it remains today although not in operational condition.

Three-coach Birdcage set No. 592 pictured here forming a train at Tonbridge on 2 August 1958. The coach nearest the camera is No. S3425S an eight-compartment 3rd brake (63ft 10½ in long overall) built by the Met.RC&W Co. in 1913 as SECR No. 1193. 63 similar three-coach sets were built between 1912 and 1915. The other coaches of the set were 1st/3rd saloon composite No. S5465S and lavatory 3rd brake No. S3497S. These sets were used widely by the Southern on local and semi-fast trains on both the Eastern and Central sections and were kept largely intact throughout their lives. They are probably the coaches most widely remembered as typical of SECR carriage stock. Some vehicles were converted for push-pull working, (see RS file No 21), but the remainder were withdrawn between 1954 and 1958. This photo therefore captures one of the very last workings of a SECR Birdcage set. [All photos David Wigley]

Double frame goods No 290 was built by Beyer Peacock in 1873 and according to Bradley survived in service until 1906 at which time it had accrued a mileage of 846,913. (According to the records of M Williams, withdrawal occurred in 1913). Whatever, the number 290 was superseded when the engine was put on the duplicate list in June 1900 and now became designated No. 0351 - later still 351A. Bradley comments that this was one of eight members of the class withdrawn in April 1906 and which were later either reinstated or used to yield spares to surviving members of the class. No 351A was destined not to run again although possibly the 1913 date refers to when the final decision was made to condemn what was left. Bereft of a number of components the remains rusted at Eastleigh for some years. Recorded here on 20 May 1920 shortly before final dismantling took place.

THE EASTLEIGH GRAVEYARD

There is something strangely appealing about a locomotive scrapyard. Many readers will recall visits to Barry or suchlike where lines of rusting machines stood silent, surplus to requirements. It is, though, all too easy to forget that this process of superseding the old in favour of the new had been taking place throughout the railway age. Barry might have signified the end and with it the transition away from steam, but in the years since much replacement and scrapping has again taken place, with so far as the Southern is concerned, the disappearance of all slam-door type trains and thus the ending of yet another era.

In the days when withdrawals were dealt with by the railway companies themselves, it was at the main workshops where lines of locomotives awaiting disposal might be found. Scrapping was also by means of dismantling - 'cutting up' in the literal sense only became possible when the technology became universal from the mid-1920s onwards.

Partly because of the time and effort it took to physically dismantle a locomotive for what was also a nominal return, it became practice for long lines of redundant machines to be stored for months, years, or even in excess of a decade before being dealt with.

The late H C Casserley visited Eastleigh several times in the years after 1920, recording a scene that appeared to change little on each occasion but one which with hindsight was a remarkable glimpse into history. Yet again I find myself wishing for time travel (and to be able to take a few spanners with me!)

*Adams 4-4-0 No. 139 (0139), shown here with its final number 0307 near the end of its life at Eastleigh on 8 May 1920.
12 engines of the type were introduced between November 1880 and January 1881. Intended at first for express duties, such was the pace of progress that despite performing well in this role, just 21 years later all had been placed on the duplicate list whilst more poignantly most were now concentrated at Eastleigh working local passenger and goods duties. (Three engines were based at Salisbury for similar work). In 1913 all were laid aside although five were found to be in better condition than some existing goods engine and as a result an obvious reinstatement / withdrawal situation occurred. No 0139 was thus numbered at this time, (an accounting problem created the need for the number change). Although recorded here in poor external condition, Bradley reports the engine was actually still on the books and not finally withdrawn until December 1924, having spent its last days on shunting duties, very local work as well as vacuum brake testing of new stock.*

Adams '46' class 4-4-2T No 124 depicted at Eastleigh on 8 May 1920. Clearly not in serviceable condition - witness the missing connecting rod as well as the smokebox door on the front framing. This was another engine officially still 'on the books' at the time but withdrawal did not take place until November 1921. It must be doubtful if it ever worked again.

The '415' class 4-4-2Ts were considered surplus to requirements from 1914 onwards and in consequence by 31 December 1920 no less than 38 of the class had congregated at Eastleigh awaiting the end. Here are Nos. 053 and 057, recorded on 8 May 1920, officially still in stock but which never worked again. Some of the engines had also been cannibalised for spares to keep others serviceable.

Two views of No. 0307 - see also page 95 - this time (above) on 16 September 1922, and below on 7 June 1924. This time there will be no reprieve, various parts having been removed whilst the boiler cladding may well have simply corroded and fallen away. The cab view below reveals that firing one of these machines might not have been that easy whilst avoiding the driver's ankles with the shovel at the same time.

Of course, not every engine in a seemingly dismantled state was condemned. Witness above 'T1' 0-4-4T No 17, recorded at the works on 17 April 1922 minus firebox, boiler and smokebox but clearly just visiting for repair. This engine remained in service until 1945.

Another engine that would survive for some time was 'A12' Jubilee No. 620, photographed on the same date as the 'T1' above and this time in an even more advanced state of dismantling. It would be reassembled and continued working until 1946.

Single-frame Beyer Goods No. 371 dated from the days of W G Beattie and had been supplied in 1878. After a life of 38 years it was laid aside in 1916 but languished, in part at least, as seen here on 14 April 1922. Other members of the class were still active into Southern railway days so it may well have been used as a source of spares.

Former '380' class 4-4-0 No 385 (renumbered 288 as seen in March 1914), already in a partly dismantled state at Eastleigh on 19 May 1923. This was another engine still, on paper at least, in stock . According to Bradley ('Wild Swan' reprint page 21), this engine, together with five others of the class, was still active in the West Country at the time of the grouping. From the illustration here such a statement must be in doubt. Again note the care taken in removing the various components. No. 0288 was officially withdrawn in August 1924.

Photographed on 19 May 1923 two years after withdrawal, '415' No 0516 reposes as a 4-4-0T in company with the remains of an unidentified Drummond 4-6-0. Again various parts are missing, the cab roof perhaps a somewhat surprising example, whilst as with a number of the engines seen on these pages the brass window surrounds appear to have disappeared fairly quickly - possibly these could be melted down easily.

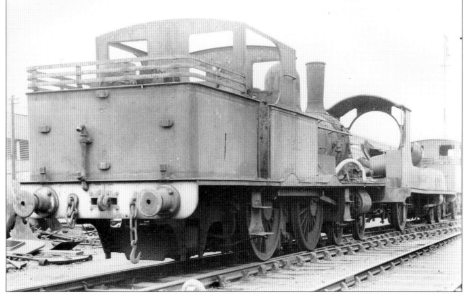

Another single framed Beyer Goods, this one No. 152 dating from 1878 and which covered just in excess of 1.1 million miles before being withdrawn in 1921. On this occasion, the safety valves, wheels and crank axle at least are missing - and again the window surrounds. Photographed on 19 May 1923.

No 160, built as '380' class 4-4-0 No. 382 in September 1879 but renumbered in January 1914. There is not really a lot of this engine left, bogie, frames and the rear driving wheel set being the principal components - the cab made of sheet metal need hardly be counted. H C Casserley recorded this image on 19 May 1923, perhaps the official withdrawal date of July 1923 referred to when the remains were finally dismembered? All 12 members of the type met their end at Eastleigh, surviving on paper at least between various dates from 1913 through to 1925. Most would appear to have covered around one million miles since being built in 1879.

On 7 June 1924 a line up of engines revealed, (from the front) Nos. 0341, 0151, 273A, 278A, 0481, 0378 and No. 0465. Below and seen from the opposite end the remains of No 0465 indicate a machine probably not long for this world - but again officially in traffic until December 1924.

We should not ignore the smaller tank engines either, above No. 0149 a '330' class 0-6-0T of 1882 recorded on 20 September 1931 a year after being laid aside. Perhaps more remarkable is the view below, this time taken on 11 September 1948 with the remains of No 332 of the same type, minus its boiler and having been withdrawn as far back as 1929.

Corrosion was slowly eating away the cab of 'Terrier' No 683 when recorded at Eastleigh on 22 September 1945. This engine had a varied career, having been built originally for the LBSCR in September 1880. It was sold out of service to the Admiralty in 1918 but by 1922 was in the Highlands working at the Dalmore Distillery, Invergordon. It travelled south to join the Shropshire & Montgomery Railway a year later in 1923, lasting there until withdrawn in 1931. After this it languished for a short time but was purchased by the Southern in 1932 as a source of spares for the numerous other 'Terriers' still operating. It is believed most of this time was spent in store at Eastleigh, during which time it naturally yielded various components but all the while becoming ever more derelict. It also managed to loose its chimney to corrosion, literally, famously snapping off as seen in the lower view on the opposite page. The remains were finally scrapped in March 1949.

Various tenders either awaiting re-use, possibly as water carriers or sludge tenders, at Eastleigh on 25 September 1932.

Unidentified remains photographed on 15 August 1937.

Two of Mr Drummond's massive but less than successful 4-6-0s of the 'G14' class, Nos. 456 and 453. Built in 1908, these machines managed an average of just 23,000 miles each year in service until withdrawn in 1925. They are seen in the Eastleigh 'Graveyard' on 16 July 1925, none of the type would be reprieved.

If the macabre fascination of withdrawn and scrapping appeals: don't forget the latest SOUTHERN WAY SPECIAL by Jeff Grayer - due in April 2013.

Further details on the inside cover of this issue of 'SW'.

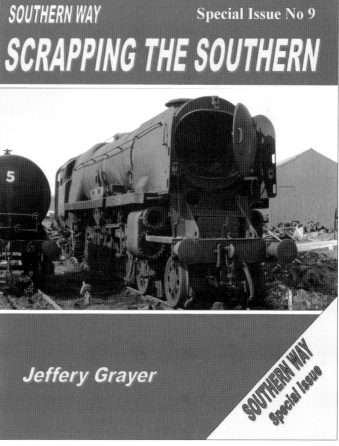

SOUTHERN WAY   Special Issue No 9

SCRAPPING THE SOUTHERN

Jeffery Grayer

SOUTHERN WAY Special Issue

KEPT IN THE DARK AT OTTERY ST MARY

Mike Green

We are all aware how for decades the railways were by default 'common carriers', meaning that they literally had to accept for conveyance anything from a cabbage to a corpse, or a mandolin to a motorcycle.

All of this traffic is now lost and with it the detail of exactly how the railways came to depend so much on revenue from goods and parcels. In the latter category much in the way of parcels traffic was despatched by passenger train, especially so on the quieter branch and cross-country routes, where perhaps except at peak times, there would be sufficient space available in the guard's compartment.

As an indication of this type of traffic, a recent purchase of the 'Goods Despatched' book from Ottery St Mary covering the period 25 April 1951 to 21 August 1952 reveals some interesting movements.

Exactly 100 transactions are covered during this time although it is interesting to note also that there were several gaps when, it appears, nothing at all was despatched. For the record in 1951 these gaps were from 5 to 29 May, 31 May to 24 June, 18 July to 7 August, 8 September to 1 October and 2 November to 23 November. Otherwise August was the busiest month with eight despatches. There was much more work in 1952 with the only gap being from 29 May to 26 June. As an example of this increase in trade, 20 items were sent out in February and 25 in April.

Generally by far the biggest user of the station was Devon Mushrooms from appropriately named nearby Devon Mushroom Farm, on occasions with multiple daily

Local working at Ottery. c.1961, BR Class 3 No 82025 enters the station from Sidmouth Junction with an Exeter to Sidmouth working. W A Camwell

despatches. Even so there were only five in 1951, between 25 June and 4 October, but in 1952 there were 36 from 4 February to 4 August. As with watercress sent elsewhere, mushrooms were despatched in containers (punnets) called 'chips' and which could weigh between 2 and 5lbs. each.

Possibly by special arrangement, railway charges were levied by consignment, rather than the destination station, therefore it does not seem possible to establish the correlation between weight, distance sent and the charge made. For example, on 16 August 1951 two consignments were sent to Exeter. One of seven chips weighing 24lbs, the other of 13 chips, recorded as weighing 1qtr 14lbs, even so both were charged at the same rate of 1/6d. But then on 3 October 1951 25 chips were sent as a single consignment weighing 3qtrs 4lbs and this time for 2/6d! Possibly there were special arrangements for particular growers as on 25 June 1951 a single chip was sent to Fowey and another to Blackburn both being charged 1/- each.

Countrywide, Birmingham was the major single destination with 80 chips sent in the 1951 period and a massive 1,789 in 1952 – clearly the area around Ottery was prime mushroom growing country. How the station staff physically coped may only be wondered as 209 chips were sent to Birmingham on 7 April, 238 on 9 May, and 205 on 4 August. Local destinations also took substantial amounts, 382 to Plymouth and 205 to Exeter.

Reverting back for a moment to 7 April 1952, the 209 sent to Birmingham were only part of the total

despatched on that occasion – we are not told by which service(s) – as the total number for the day was actually 279, closely followed by 269 on 4 August. The lowest despatch for a day was just five on 17 July 1951, two to nearby Budleigh Salterton and three to Birmingham. Trains on the branch were normally two-coach sets, apart from when through coaches were added at holiday times, so did this mean that the station master at Ottery would advise Exeter an extra van might be required on a particular day – assuming he was given notice of course? Three days of typical despatches are shown below.

Not mentioned in the main text above was that mushrooms were sent not just to the places previously mentioned but to such varied destinations as Crediton, Comrie and Perth, although we may wonder how long it took to get Scotland let alone Blackburn and what state they were in when they arrived!

Apart from fungi, other goods were also despatched from the station, and formed a totally bizarre mix. In total there were around sixty 'miscellaneous' entries with those below as a representative selection. (Locally it has been rumoured that day-old chicks were another regular traffic but there does not appear to be any evidence of this, unless, that is, the entry for 30 August 1951 applies but it might perhaps appear somewhat heavy.) Note also that a weight for a despatch is not always shown in the book.

It is possible that the register found is only one out

Date	Destination	No	Description	Weight			Total		
				Cwts	Qtrs	Lbs	£	s	d
04/10/51	Exmouth	1	Chip Mushrooms			2		1	0
	Exeter	8	Chips ditto		1	0		1	6
	Teignmouth	1	Chip ditto			5		1	2
	Birmingham	16	Chips ditto		1	24		6	7
	Exeter	25	Chips ditto		3	0		1	6
								11	9

Date	Destination	No	Description	Weight			Total		
				Cwts	Qtrs	Lbs	£	s	d
14/02/52	Teignmouth	1	Chip Mushrooms			4		1	3
	Exmouth	1	Chip ditto			3		1	1
	Plymouth	8	Chips ditto			26		3	11
	Birmingham	58	Chips ditto	1	2	26	1	2	10
							1	9	1

Date	Destination	No	Description	Weight			Total		
				Cwts	Qtrs	Lbs	£	s	d
30/06/52	Plymouth	30	Chips Mushrooms		3	9		7	3
	Fowey	1	Chip ditto			4		1	3
	Exeter	20	Chips ditto		2	11		2	0
	Budleigh Salterton	10	Chips ditto		1	6		1	8
	Blackburn	1	Chip ditto			2		1	1
	Birmingham	17	Chips ditto		1	22		7	3
							1	0	6

An afternoon Exmouth to Sidmouth Junction train exchanges the tablet at Ottery, 5 September 1964. Services were withdrawn on the line on 6 March 1967.
Andrew Muckley

KEPT IN THE DARK AT OTTERY ST MARY

Date	Destination	No	Description	Weight			Total		
				Cwts	Qtrs	Lbs	£	s	d
25/04/51	Wimbledon		Chains		1	19		11	3
03/05/51	Starcross	1	Packet			6		1	3
04/05/51	London	1	Battery			21		3	8
12/07/51	St Albans	3	Cartons		3	2		14	2
17/08/51	London (Phillips)	1	Wireless in Carton			27		9	7
20/08/51	A Dealer in Sandford	1	Ditto		1	1		3	11
30/08/51	London	2	Boxes of Poultry	1	2	25		16	10
06/09/51	London	1	Box	1	0	26	1	12	2
09/10/51	Waterloo	1	Parcel of Clothing			12		3	0
02/01/52	Manchester	2	Cartons		1	12		8	9
19/02/52	Plymouth (Dunlop)	1	Tyre					1	8
20/03/52	Haslemere	1	Trunk	1	2	17	1	19	6
24/03/52	Holt Norfolk	1	Bicycle				1	4	1
01/04/52	Bristol (Brown Bros)	1	Pram					11	9
06/05/52	Birmingham	1	Parcel			12		3	11
	To same address	1	Ditto			14		4	11
20/05/52	London	1	Hamper					9	2
21/05/52	Chichester	4	Packages		2	24	1	1	7
28/05/52	Boreham (RNLI)	1	Carton		1	2		5	1
02/07/52	Chadwell Heath	1	R/C Box					1	3
15/08/52	Royston	2	Boxes		1	24		3	8

of two or more, as there appear to be only two items of Passengers Luggage in Advance. One, a case sent to Felling on Tyne on 8 August 1951 and a portmanteau sent to Sidcup on the 25th of the same month. Both were charged at 4/-. Three items in the record seem most unusual and are listed below. All were endorsed as 'At Consignees Risk' and there were four receipts for items to be delivered. These are also listed below.

Presumably the dogs were in a wooden box or crate but what arrangements were made for their welfare during the journey? Intriguingly also, why was a box of fish being sent to Grimsby? A case of 'coals to Newcastle'.

So there you have it, an insight to what life was like in the Parcels Office of a country station in Devon. I do not comment on whether the activity was cost effective, just an example of what life was like at Ottery station 60 years ago.

(For those unfamiliar with pre-decimal terms: 1 Ton = 20 hundredweights (cwts). 1 hundredweight = 4 quarters (qtrs). 1 Quarter = 28 pounds (lbs). In currency a pound (£) = 20 shillings(s). One shilling = 12 pennies (d). Normally expressed as £1/1/1d for example.)

Date	Destination	No	Description	Weight			Total		
				Cwts	Qtrs	Lbs	£	s	d
30/05/51	Grimsby. For the London Central Meal Co	1	Box of Fish			4		3	1
05/12/51	Roydon	1	Dog in a Box	1	0	18	1	10	4
10/12/51	Scunthorpe	1	ditto	1	0	25	1	18	4

The following were reported as being sent as 'consignee's risk':

Date	Destination	No	Description	Weight			Total		
				Cwts	Qtrs	Lbs	£	s	d
07/09/51	Warcop	1	Parcel		1	21		8	5
17/10/51	Waterloo	1	Hamper		1	17		10	11
28/11/51	Grantham	1	Toy Wheelbarrow			6		2	5

Few items were reported as being received, although these were noted:

Date	Destination	No	Description	Weight			Total		
				Cwts	Qtrs	Lbs	£	s	d
08/02/52	Devon Mushroom Co	1	Tarpaulin					2	0
		2	Boxes						
31/03/52	Private	1	Box					7	7
24/04/52	ditto		Fencing					1	3
09/05/52	ditto	3	Containers					2	8

0-6-2T 'Kitchener' crossing the original No 6 bridge on the approach to Longmoor with a train from Liss. The lines underneath fan out to form the locomotive yard, where much covered accommodation was available. The bridge structure was replaced in the early 1950s. At this time it will be noted that the ends of the bridge rested on timber trestles. The girders and supports were replaced in 1952, the former now resting on masonry piers.

REMEMBER LONGMOOR?

Images from the collection of Les Burberry

The Longmoor Military Railway, or from the outset more accurate the Woolmer Instructional Military Railway has its origins in 1903 when an 18" tramway was laid to assist in the removal of some 70 corrugated iron huts from the existing military camp at Longmoor 3½ miles to Bordon.

Between 1905 and 1907 the railway was relaid to standard gauge it being extended several times until at its peak consisted over 70 miles operations track and sidings.

The route was basically south to north, forming a junction with the Portsmouth direct line at Liss to a further connection with the national network at Bordon, the latter a branch terminus off the LSWR Farnham to Alton line at Bentley. Perhaps the LMR's most interesting feature was a complete circular course from Longmoor around to Whitehill and back again. Numerous odd sidings and depots, including one rejoicing with the delightful name of 'Apple Pie', were scattered around and soldiers could literally 'play trains' although as this was the military the whole was of course taken very seriously. Conventional stock was used and it must be admitted the training given and expertise gained were of immeasurable use in various conflicts over the years.

Sadly, economic cuts and with it the statement that railways were not considered to be as vital as they once were meant the end of the LMR from 1969. In its last couple of years it had taken on the role of a preservation centre, 'Blackmore Vale', 'Clan Line' David Shepherds's two engines and others finding, what would sadly turn out to be temporary homes amidst the Hampshire countryside.

Longmoor made for the perfect preservation centre, BR access, no nearby housing and plenty of room together with engineering facilities on site. Unfortunately a group of well-heeled locals, particularly in the area around Liss were determined to stop grown men playing with their train set. The result was an ugly confrontation, one incident recalled by the owner of a steam engine temporarily standing near an access path who was threatened by a local in her Morris 1000 with the words, "If you don't move that ****** I will ram it." Shades of the Titfield Thunderbolt, although farcical when considering a few hundredweight against many tons.

At the time Longmoor was one of two embryonic preservation centres in Hampshire - the other was at Droxford - the Mid Hants was some years in the future.

Today all vestige of track has been removed, some of the track bed given over to roadway whilst the A3 trunk road rushes past Longmoor where the military still reside, albeit minus railway.

The now preserved 2-10-0 'Gordon' at Longmoor Downs platform. This was one of two engines of the type on the line in 1963 although others had certainly been present in earlier years.

Above - *Operational railway working was taught using a model railway complete with locking frame and requisite block instruments. Besides double line working, there was also a tablet instrument for single line and 'telephone and ticket' working. Model equipment varied over the years but included the products of Bassett– Lowke and later original Hornby. 'Stations' included Slough, Whitehill, Windsor, Woolmer and Oakhanger. The prominence of GWR names will be noted, indeed the original military railway maintained excellent relations with the GWR for which reason Spagnoletti type 'pegging' block instruments were originally provided, although by the time the view was taken (undated) these had been replaced with more conventional rotary blocks. One GWR remnant remains in the form of the signal repeater at the far left end of the block shelf. Trains were 'driven' by the instructor from a console in the middle of the room and followed the indication given by the trainee 'blockman'.*

Right - *'Hawthorn Leslie 0-6-2T 'Sir John French' was supplied new to the military in 1914 but transferred to the Kinmel Camp Railway (located near Rhyl in North Wales) in 1916. The engine returned to Longmoor sometime after 1917 and survived until 1946. From the designation 'W.I.M.R,' on the front coach - an ex GWR 'Toplight' it is likely the view was taken either during or shortly after WW1. The leading coach also carries the designation 'Kitchen' on the first set of opening double doors. This engine is known to have been fully overhauled at Eastleigh in 1936 which included a repaint in lined green Southern type livery.*

Opposite page - *Former LBSCR 'I2' tank engines, LBSCR Nos 13 and 19 of 1908, respectively SR Nos 2013 and 2019 photographed out of use in September 1948. Acquired by the railway in 1939 and 1937, they appear to have been used solely on the LMR but were evidently not considered much use post-war as both were reported languishing in sidings by 1947. It was the practice on the LMR to use old stock for rerailing exercises (at other times rerailing became an unplanned necessity) so they may very well have been towed to various parts of the route during this sojourn. By 1950 both had been sold for scrap, reposing at Guildford for a time on their way to the cutter's yard. Notice the interesting chimney cover on WD 72401.*

Above - *As has been seen, coaching stock on the line was mainly in the form of ex-main line vehicles, and included examples from the GWR, LSWR and SECR. In the last-named category was included a pair of 'Birdcage' brakes, at times operated with the brake compartment ends coupled together as a two-coach train. (In later years the former GWR vehicles were reported as having been modified internally with modern plastic seating over a tubular metal frame.) Of the LSWR vehicles, one served as an Ambulance coach.*

Don't forget the excellent book recently released by our friends at Lightmoor Press and highly recommended.

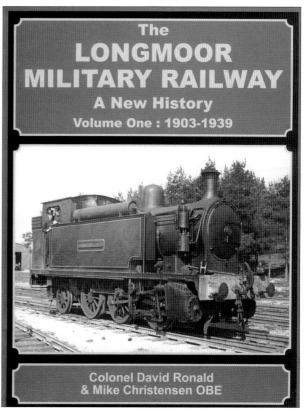

The
LONGMOOR MILITARY RAILWAY
A New History
Volume One : 1903-1939

Colonel David Ronald
& Mike Christensen OBE

'REBUILT' - THE LETTERS AND COMMENTS PAGES

We start with a bit of a catch-up and not in any particular order. Not sure everything will fit, but if I keep quiet it might just! So from Jeremy Clarke reference No 21. "I haven't had a chance to do more than glance through it yet but the photo of No 40 (p53) is interesting in that the 'gimcrack' Stroudley rolling stock illustrated was still trundling along the SLL almost until the time the Brighton decided to electrify the line (1903, completed 1909). Perhaps this shows why that decision was taken! The LBSCR usually took photos of its stock on the Crumbles line at Eastbourne, generally also in reverse of this one with the south-facing nearside closest to the camera. The trackwork in the foreground of this shot does not, to my recollection, appear in any others actually noted as being at Crumbles, which suggests this is taken elsewhere. No 40 herself had a mixed existence: born March 1878, exhibited in Paris that year and awarded a gold medal, a fact publicised on the tank sides for several years: sold to the Isle of Wight Central Railway in January 1902 (obviously no sentiment in LBSCR Loco dept!) which numbered her 11: rebuilt to A1X in August 1918: Southern added 'W' to number in 1923 and name 'Newport' in MacLeod era: returned to mainland February 1947 to become 2640 and then 32640 in 1948: withdrawn September 1963. Now back in the Isle of Wight at Havenstreet."

In No 21, page 41, we also raised the question on 'What is that third coach?' Fortunately there are those out there with the required knowledge, including Raymond Butt. "Easy peasy! To put it simply, it is an example of the most comfortable pre-grouping coach I have ever ridden in, despite its peculiar exterior appearance. I only travelled in one once, and then only between Peterborough (North, as it then was) and Grantham. It is, of course, one of the 'Barnum' series, with lovely recessed doors and beautiful curly grab handles at the ends of the vehicle (certainly in the case of the one I travelled in - possibly only a few had them - they also had the first example I had ever come across of a saloon with tables with flaps which folded over (like the Eurostar tables) to enable passengers occupying the window seats to get in and out relatively comfortably. Exterior and interior photographs of the 'Barnums' appear pp.309/10 of George Dow's *Great Central*, Vol 3. (Ian Allan 1965)".

A second note from Mr Butt yielded yet more, "Looking in more detail at the photographs in Dow's book, there are features about the doors on the 'Barnum' saloons which are unique, and about which I had quite forgotten. Whereas those on 'Barnum' compartment stock were in one way unusual, those on the saloon stock certainly were - and on two counts. Firstly, instead of just one window per door, the 'Barnum' saloon doors had two quarterlights and two toplights; secondly, and more remarkably (and probably uniquely) instead of being opened and closed by means of a door-handle, they had a *door-knob* - entry into a 'Barnum' saloon which was like entering the hallway of an Edwardian villa!

"It appears to me that the saloon illustrated in SW21 is probably one *without* the curly grab-handles which I remember and to which I previously referred. The fact that the doors are recessed renders them invisible as seen from the angle at which the photograph was taken, giving the coach the appearance of being a doorless vehicle!"

Peter Tatlow provides similar information plus detail of the initial make-up of the train, "Page 41, top: The Adams X6 No. 663 hauling the train Newcastle to Bournemouth has behind it the following, Gresley 8 compartment corridor third, probably ex-ECJS, some of which were transferred to the GC Section by the LNER / LNER Gresley 4 compartment corridor brake third / ex-GC

Left - Bulleid 'Merchant Navy' tender recorded at Eastleigh in 1946, certainly not new, as witness the torn roof canvas. Notice also the alternative water filler, it saved the crew from mounting the rear of the tender but possibly meant the risk of a soaking on the footplate. Did any of those gunmetal 'Southern' plates survive?

Opposite page - 'P' class 0-6-0T No 31556 at Hodson's Mill Robertsbridge in 1962. Ross Shimmon. (Ross is the Editor of 'The Colonel' of the 'Colonel Stephens Society').

open third saloon Barnum stock / beyond this is difficult to tell, but the shorter coaches just might be ex-GC Parker stock."

Now to Issue 20 and a note from John Raggett. (At the time of his note John commented he was touring Australia and New Zealand last autumn and was worried I had missed this edition.) "I note the letter from Derek Taylor about level crossings. Stone me, Stone Crossing on the North Kent, right on my door step! It was also on my core route for route knowledge when I was learning to drive trains a few years ago, Hither Green to Hoo Junction being our depot core route for trainees. You had to produce your own route map to demonstrate route learning skills and I even visited this crossing as part of the exercise. However, the point I was making was about public level crossings. Shornmead Crossing is indeed a gated crossing but not a public one and although it used to have side gates for pedestrians, there is no public right of way. Shornmead used to have a crossing keeper but his job had been done away with by the time I went to Hoo Junction in 1993. There were safety issues then about DOO freight trains setting back over the crossing and Network Rail finally sealed up the pedestrian gates in 2010.

"Littlehaven crossing, one of only two where the gates were worked by capstan wheel inside the cabin, has just been converted to barriers. The other is Plumpton Gates in Sussex. This leaves ten public crossings with gates on the former Southern: Rushton and Stoke, both on the Wessex side in Dorset, Stone Crossing, Grain, Cuxton, East Farleigh, Wateringbury, Chartham and Wye in Kent and Plumpton in Sussex. There is one other manned, gated crossing, at Havensmouth, Normans Bay in east Sussex, but this is not a public crossing."

Now from John Burgess concerning the 'Over and Under' feature in SW20. "If you can forgive me for having yet another twopenny worth, perhaps I can add some comments relating to the photograph on the top of page 68

showing Coppins Bridge at Newport. The view has been published several times previously, but I have never seen any other photographs of this location from the ground which surprises me, as the bridge spans the main road from Ryde into Newport and must have been very familiar to many. The bridge as depicted was built by the impoverished Isle of Wight (Newport Junction) Railway which had opened its line from Sandown to a temporary Newport terminus at Pan Lane a short distance to the south early in February 1875, but it took over four years to complete the short section from there into the main station at Newport largely because the railway company was more or less bankrupt and could not raise the capital to construct the bridges and viaduct. Coppins Bridge had a span of 110 feet

The Brighton line platforms at Lewes looking east. WD No 77101 runs through with ecs from Polegate destined for Brighton. 10 June 1950.

S C Nash

and gained some notoriety with local people, some of whom refused to travel over this section of line for fear that the bridge would collapse. It is possible that the two cast iron columns were added at a later date to strengthen the structure.

The bridge was replaced in 1920 and it is possible that the view shows preliminary work in connection with this - judging from the ladder and the block and tackle, something is going on.

The freight train on the bridge is also very interesting as it shows wagons on either side of the locomotive. It is possible that the wagon at the bunker end had been collected from sidings at the Pan Lane Mill where the connection faced trains approaching from the Sandown direction or alternatively this wagon and others out of shot might have been picked up from the chalk quarry at Shide. Loaded wagons from there were regularly propelled to the cement mill about a mile to the north of Newport on the

Cowes line. These wagons were privately owned and during Southern Railway days were acquired by Blue Circle and painted a striking yellow colour.

My curiosity about the later appearance of the bridge led me to have a go at sketching the scene in oils, using the photograph plus an image showing the bridge under construction in the Metropolitan Carriage works in Wednesbury, I attempted a view showing a cement train being propelled over the bridge during the 1930s. A further view of the location after the line had closed and the bridge had been removed was found on the net, and I used this for a second view from a slightly different viewpoint showing a typical passenger train from the early or mid 1950s with an O2 hauling a couple of ex SECR carriages. In this photograph the white painted shop has 'Lucky Dip' rather crudely sign written on its end, but in acknowledgment of the help in referencing some of the history in my view this has become Maycock and Silsbury Books, whose series of

118

volumes on the Isle of Wight provides the most comprehensive set of histories of these lines that I have discovered. The only other reference I had at the time were a few grainy frames of home cine film shot from a train approaching the bridge from the south in the 1950s, which helped me to show the viaduct and the background structures. Since completing the sketches, I have found two views of the bridge taken from trains in Mike Jacobs' book 'Memories of Isle of Wight Railways' which you published in 2010, but still nothing from ground level. I should add that this part of Newport has changed out of all recognition as a result of road construction and other redevelopment and my views are unrecognisable on the ground today."

No 20 certainly appears to have created some comment - we don't do it intentionally. This from Roger Merry-Price, "Regarding the photo of N15X No. 32328 at Basingstoke on page 77. The LNER beaver-tail observation car was at Basingstoke waiting to be shunted onto the rear of the 18:30 return excursion from Farnborough to Leeds Central (Service No. 290). The stock for the excursion had berthed at Woking whilst the passengers visited the Farnborough Air Show. For some reason it was routed in the up direction from Woking (at 17:10) before taking a left turn at Byfleet Junction, another left turn at Virginia Water and another at Ascot before turning right at Frimley Junction over the now closed and lifted spur and back on to the down main line. Arrival at Farnborough was scheduled for 18:20, with 18:30 the booked departure. Arrival at Basingstoke was scheduled for 18:50. Presumably the SR locomotive was taken off and then the observation car was

coupled up whilst a WR locomotive was coupled up at the Reading end. Departure from Basingstoke was scheduled for 19:05 and the train was booked at Southcote Junction at 19:28."

Roger also add a further gem again from No. 20. "Regarding the photograph on the bottom of page 44. I suspect the train is the 11.35 from Victoria to Ramsgate, the formation of which consisted of a BR Standard 4 car set with 2 Pullmans in between. I accept the photo shows three Pullmans rather than two but from my own personal observation at Whitstable in the 1958/9 period there were a number of occasions when an extra car was added."

Long time supporter Viv Orchard adds further to the comments on SW20 - he quite rightly points out we had failed to identify the location of the cover image of No 20. It is of course Guildford from the camera of Roger Thornton.

"Another fine edition. So much of interest and new. I could not find a description of the cover picture but it looks remarkably like Guildford by the coaling shed with the Civil Engineers depot and blacksmith's forge in the background, sadly all now a car park. I take some exception to the guest editorial in so much that here on the Isle of Wight we have the actual Paris Exposition Gold Medal Engine. We are well aware of the exploits in Paris with Westinghouse demonstrating their air brake systems around the Suburban lines. It is now an A1X class but I still think that if it was fitted with dummy wing plates, dual braked and painted with the Gold Medal livery there would be many preserved railways that would wish to hire it and capitalise upon its history. Further, why not take it to Paris

From Dave Richards this view of the goods yard at Oakley almost in the very last days of operation - see also SW No. 8.

and run it again around the Suburban lines? The history is not destroyed and it would be patently clear that it was no longer an A or A1. Tragically, to get others to see the benefits of such an exercise with its considerable historical and financial rewards to all, is virtually impossible. That interesting picture on page 55 of an electric motor coach hauling wagons will be a wonderful excuse for any one with a model railway! I assume it could only happen with this type of motor coach because it has two motor bogies with the attendant horse power. The picture on page 69 refers to check rails. Those on the outside of the track are guard rails and are to prevent any derailed vehicle remaining within the confines of the bridge structure. They are not to keep wheels on rails due to curvature of the track. Finally, the picture on page 78 illustrates, I assume, testing the brickwork in the crown. Keep up the good work." (We will try!)

And that I regret is all we do have space for this time, more in No 23 as I have promised Bill Allan I would leave room for his three colour views of E1s on tour.

COLOUR INTERLUDE by Bill Allan

*Top -*Hardham Junction, south of Pulborough, and the LCGB "The Sussex Coast Limited" is about to leave the main line and traverse the Midhurst branch. It is 24 June 1962 and the two radials E4 Nos. 32503 and E6 32417 have taken over the train at Horsham from the preserved T9 120. Brighton shed cleaners have done a grand job preparing the tanks. No. 32417 appears elsewhere in this issue on more mundane duties. E4 No. 32503 entered traffic in 1900, named 'Buckland', and was first shedded at Brighton. Post-war Tonbridge (74D) became the locomotive's base until 1955 when it returned to Brighton. Finally it was withdrawn as one of the last survivors in April 1963.

Centre and bottom - The E6 and E4 return from Midhurst, bunker first leaving the branch at Hardham Junction. Thanks to "The Railtour Files" and timings recorded by John Clifford, we know it is 1.37 pm. My father remembered the whole day as nearly perfect with bright sun and heat! Traces of the line remain today as a track bed. The place where the photo was taken is close to the Hardham tunnel of the Wey and Arun canal which burrowed under the line. As and when the restoration of "London's Lost Route to the Sea" is completed it is unlikely that the tunnel will be re-instated. An E4 from Horsham shed and latterly Three Bridges on Duty 693 was regularly used in the 1950s on the 7.25 am goods Horsham – Midhurst arriving at 10.25 am – then after shunting and a visit as required to the Brick Company's siding the goods meandered back to Horsham. Timings were 12.30 pm depart Midhurst arriving back in Horsham at 4.2 pm, a leisurely trip for engine and crew. When Midhust closed the service continued for a while to Petwoth until final closure and lifting of the branch. Petworth station survives as a superior Bed and Breakfast initially restored in one of those strange coincidences by a friend from Dental School days Mike Rapley and his wife Lou. They sold it later but not before rescuing Pullman carriages from Cornwall as extra accommodation. As for Midhurst – sadly the whole site has disappeared under housing! Perhaps a ghostly E4 is occasionally heard in someone's living room!